Stories That Live
The Parables of Jesus

Gary L. Carver

Parson's Porch & Company

Parson's Porch Books

Stories That Live: The Parables of Jesus

ISBN: Softcover 978-1-951472-85-6

Copyright © 2014 by Gary L. Carver

All rights reserved. No part of this book may be reproduced or transmitted in any form or by any means, electronic or mechanical, including photocopying, recording, or by any information storage and retrieval system, without permission in writing from the publisher.

To order additional copies of this book, contact:

Parson's Porch Books

1-423-475-7308

www.parsonsporch.com

Parson's Porch Books is an imprint of Parson's Porch & Company (PP&C) in Cleveland, Tennessee. PP&C is an innovative non-profit organization which raises money by publishing books of noted authors, representing all genres. All donations from contributors and profits from publishing are shared with the poor.

Stories That Live
The Parables of Jesus

Table of Contents

Preface	9
A Life that Lasts Matthew 7:24-27	13
Gonna Lay My Burdens Down Matthew 11:16-19	18
Rush to Judgment Matthew 13:24-30	22
The Trouble with Evil Matthew 13:24-30	26
And the Winner Is Matthew 13:24-30	33
Sorting Out Wheat and Weeds Matthew 13:24-30	38
Be Influential Matthew 13:33-45	43
When Is It OK not to be a Christian? Matthew 18:23-35	48
Unless You Forgive Matthew 18:23-35	53
Grumbling over Generosity Matthew 20:1-16	58
Unfair! Matthew 20:1-16	63
Grumbling About Grace Matthew 20:1-16	67

The Longest Journey   73
    Matthew 21:28-30

R.S.V.P.   78
    Matthew 22:1-14

Be Prepared   83
    Matthew 25:1-13

What to do During the Delay   87
    Matthew 25:1-13

The Rich Get Richer   93
    Matthew 25:14-30

What Are You Doing with What You've Got?   98
    Matthew 25:14-30

Who Takes the Responsibility?   103
    Matthew 25:14-30

When Judgment is Good   109
    Matthew 25:31-46

Sometimes You Never Know!   113
    Matthew 25:31-46

The Least of These   118
    Matthew 25:31-46

A Good Neighbor   122
    Luke 10:25-37

How to Get to Heaven   128
    Luke 10:25-37

The Original Prayer   134
    Luke 11:5-8

Faithfully Claiming the Future   139
    Luke 12:16-21

Cost Analysis 　　Luke 14:28-32	143
Amazing (and Offensive) Grace 　　Luke 15:11-32	147
Waiting on the Porch 　　Luke 16:19-31	151
Believing the Bible 　　Luke 16:19-31	156
I Wanna Big Faith 　　Luke 17:7-10	162
When You Are About to Quit 　　Luke 18:1-8	167
Press On! 　　Luke 18:1-8	171
It's Not about Me 　　Luke 18:9-14	176
A Storyteller's Story	181

Preface

These are thirty-six sermons hammered out on the hard anvil of life lived with a local community of faith.

Sometimes a preaching minister is overwhelmed with the inspiration of having something to say. Sometimes a preaching minister is overwhelmed by the responsibility of having to say something. These sermons fall into the category of the later. They were forged from the constant experience of having to answer the bell to preach each Lord's Day regardless of circumstance. They were fashioned from the background of 49 years in the pastorate and six years with this particular congregation, one that presents to the proclaimer the pressure of knowing good preaching whether they hear it from me or not.

There is no consistent style or form to these sermons. Each sermon draws its substance and form from the experience of its respective text, as did the worship services in which they were proclaimed. The nature of these sermons is more inductive than deductive as were, of course, the parables from which they came. A conscientious effort was made to prepare and present these sermons in a way as to preserve the oral nature of preaching as well as the nature of the parable itself. The congregation at worship was invited to "hear" the scriptural texts and the sermons were delivered without a manuscript. These manuscripts were taken off of a vocal tape and edited.

One quickly will note that there often are several different sermons preached on the same parable. Hopefully, this will preserve the integrity of the arena of interpretation as well as applying its truth to different situations at different times.

I want to thank my dear friend, David Tullock, for his gracious invitation to submit these messages for publication. I am particularly grateful to Dr. Tullock for the invitation to write about the parables of Jesus.

Jesus was no closet recluse or ivory tower philosopher. His unforgettable stories stuck in the minds of his listeners because he lived with and among them. They reflect his genius for understanding the reality and complexity of everyday life. They teach us about a life lived to its fullest, a life like no other, the very life of Jesus himself, which he wants to share with us, even today. Thus the title, *Stories that Live*.

I wish to express my deepest gratitude to the family of faith at the First Cumberland Presbyterian Church of Chattanooga, the best church of which I know. To be called to this wonderful congregation at age 62 was a grace gift of God, one of which I could never be worthy. In many ways, God saved the best for last.

I also want to express my sincere thankfulness to the staff and worship team at First Cumberland: Bruce Clark, Jenni Faires, Charles Mitchell, Gerald Peel, Sam and Sarah Quattrochi and Danny Williams. Their insight, creativity and partnership in ministry have made this a better book and me a better minister.

Heartfelt thanks goes to Tammi Long and Janice Guider who have poured countless hours to the task of preparing this manuscript as well as giving wise counsel and unlimited patience. It would not have happened without them.

Especially, I want to thank my loving wife and partner, for 49 years, Sharlon, who 17 years ago urged me to write my first book and 6 books later still is my strength and encourager. In this book, she and I both want to acknowledge the companionship of a little one who will never read it, Saban Zoe.

We also want to dedicate this book to four wonderful expression of serendipitous joy, our grandchildren, Brandon, Katelyn, Hadley and Alyssa. Without becoming overly sentimental, I want to express my gratitude to my Lord Jesus, whose stories these were initially, whose love and sacrifice changed my life and whose life still lives in me.

Bill Bright, founder of Campus Crusade, was once asked to describe his personal relationship to his Lord, Jesus. He stopped, became very still, sat and simply cried. I think I know a little of that which he felt.

Dedicated to

Brandon Murphy Carver
Katelyn Davis Carver
Hadley Elizabeth Carver
Alyssa Davis Carver
The epitome of serendipitous Joy!

A LIFE THAT LASTS!
Matthew 7: 24-27

J. Wallace Hamilton was a great preacher of another generation. He wrote a book entitled *What About Tomorrow* and in that book he tells the story of a wealthy builder. The wealthy builder called his top assistant, a man with whom he had a long relationship, and said, "I am going away for about ten months, and I want for you to oversee the building of my house because when I return I am intending to retire ... quickly."

After he left, the assistant began to think, if he retires what is going to happen to me? Besides he has not done that much for me anyway. He did oversee the building of the house, but yet at every opportunity he had, he feathered his own nest. He hired an immoral builder, hired inferior workers and bought inferior products. He was always cutting and overcharging and pocketing the extra amount. Oh, it looks good on the outside, but on the inside the flaws are very apparent and it is also very assured that the house would not stand the ravages of time or the ways of nature. In ten months the builder returns and says, "Does it not look pretty?" "Yes, it does." says the top assistant. "Does it not look beautiful?" "Yes, it does." "Well, I got to thinking about you and I am going to retire in a couple of years and I wanted to see that you would be taken care of. The house is yours."

It is a clear point. We are all building the house in which we live. We all are building the life that we live today, tomorrow and yes, to some extent, the Bible says throughout all eternity we are today building the house that we will live in the rest of lives and from now on.. It reminds us of the statement of the man who said, "If I had known I would live this long, I would have taken better care of myself." We all feel that way. But it is true the house we are building today is the house we will live in today, tomorrow and to some extent even forever.

It is not by accident that this parable is played at the end of the great Sermon on the Mount; the greatest gathering of ethical and moral teachings ever in the history of our planet. It is almost as if this parable is a summation; an exclamation point to the entire Sermon oil the Mount. We sometimes must remember the Sermon on the Mount is prescriptive, yes. It tells us all what we should and must do. But it is also descriptive. It is descriptive in the sense that this is the kind of life one leads. These are the things that one does when he or she has the firm foundation which is Jesus Christ our Lord. It is the way we naturally live our lives out of that which Christ has placed within us as we acknowledge him as Lord and Savior. So then, how can we better build a life that last? How can we better build a house in which we will be living from now on?

One, I think we simply begin with a sure foundation. Jesus told about two builders; one built upon sand and the other built upon rock. We know the results. The inevitable storms came and the house upon the sand crashed and the one upon the rock did not. It is a great temptation, even today, to build our lives upon the sand of the quick fix - the easy religion, the cheap grace! Sit in front of the TV. Send in a dollar and we will be anointed with some kind of anointing on high. The easy way! Run to the answer men. Run to those who already have it figured out and they will tell you exactly everything to do. You bear no responsibilities. You simply do what they say. In fact the Sermon on the Mount talks about just the opposite. The greatest writing probably on the Sermon on the Mount was by Dietrich Bonhoeffer entitled *The Cost of Discipleship* in which he warns-us against a cheap grace. There are some commentators that feel the seventh chapter the twelfth verse is really the climax of the Sermon on the Mount. You know that verse. You memorized it as a child. "Do unto others as you would have them do unto you." When we live a life that is founded upon the Lord Jesus Christ and let his spirit and love flow in and through us we then treat everyone else as we wish to be treated. It is the very summation of the entire Sermon on the Mount.

And then the Lord Jesus Christ, in Matthew, gives us three warnings. Number one: you can't do this if you go through the broad gate. That broad gate leads to destruction. You must go through the narrow gate. The narrow gate of obedience. The narrow gate of discipline. And as we go through that narrow gate of discipline and obedience we will be on our way to demonstrating what the Sermon on the Mount is about. He then gives us another warning about false prophets. False prophets! He never condemns what the false prophets say. He condemns what the false prophet does. For you see the false prophet is one who says one thing and does another. He is one whose life is inconsistent. One whose life is fragmented. One who is a hypocrite. The one who teaches one thing and the teaching may be good, but yet ones life reflects something else. And then he summarizes it with this marvelous parable by saying, "She that hears and does my word is like one who builds ones house upon the rock." We begin with the sure foundation. We build our lives upon Jesus Christ, Himself. We build our life upon His words, His thoughts, His actions, the way He lived life.

It was in the 1850's, I think, that a pastor who had become a Christian late in life still yet young in the faith by the name of Edward Mote who not only expressed his new found faith in his sermons, but through poetry. One day he had been piddling and toying with a poem several verses of which he had written when he went to call on one of his parishioners on a Sunday afternoon. There he found that parishioner was on her death bed and he thought of the poem that he had within his pocket. He took out the poem and gave it to the woman and it was a word for her dying. It was a word for our living because those words by Edward Mote said,

> My hope is built on nothing less
> Than Jesus blood and righteousness.
> I dare not trust the sweetest frame,
> But wholly lean on Jesus name.
> On Christ the solid rock I stand.
> All other ground is sinking sand.
> All other ground is sinking sand."

So we begin to build our life on that strong foundation of our personal faith and commitment and then we begin to build with balance. We build with balance. There is a congruity between our saying and our doing - the life we confess and the life that we live. There is no easy religion. There is no quick fix. It is only known through the discipline of knowing and doing. The obedience of the caring and doing.

This past week I was privileged to hear one of our very finest of preachers, Dr. Joel Gregory. As you know, he was not only a famous professor of preaching who later went to occupy the pulpit of the First Baptist Church of Dallas where after a short period of time he fell from that pulpit. He sold cemetery plots for the ten years and has been the publisher of a magazine. He was a powerful, eloquent, articulate pulpiteer. He preached that day and said, "Beware of quick success. Beware of the quick and sometimes easy road." And then he said of himself, "The presence of one gift took me to a place where the absence of other gifts would not let me stay."

G. K. Chesterton said, "Nothing quite fails like success." 'There is no easy path. There is no quick way. There is no special anointing. There is no exercising of a gift that all of a sudden we are a spiritually superior Christian. It just doesn't happen in the Lord's way of doing things. Horace Greeley was once sent a letter by a woman who said, "Save our church. Save our church! Help us to save our church from financial straits. We have tried a raffle. We have tried a bazaar. We have even tried a strawberry festival" And then she went on to describe other things that they had tried. Horace Greeley's words to her were, "Try Christianity." That is how we build a life that lasts. That is how great churches are built. We go back to the very, very basics of what God has called us to do. The very, very basics of our faith.

Your life in our church would be revolutionized if every single one of us did three simple things: personal worship, financial responsibility, and the sharing of our faith. Personal worship: If every member of First Baptist Church spent thirty minutes per day in personal worship to the Lord Jesus Christ (many of you already do that). But what if every person did? What if every person did the simple basics of reading our Bibles, prayer, meditation, and journaling thirty minutes a day?

Financial responsibility! Many of you already do this. You already tithe. But what if every member of First Cumberland Church tithed? What if half of the membership of First Cumberland Church tithed? You already know the joy and benefits of it, but what if everybody did that? You say, "Well I can't tithe right now." For some of you that means you start giving anything. For others that might mean giving ten dollars more a week. Do you realize what it would mean if every family, every member, every person or giving unit in First Cumberland Church gave ten dollars a week more? That is barely above the cost of a coke a day. We would not have any financial problems.

Thirdly, if every single one of us at least once a week made a conscientious effort to share our faith - invite someone to church, perform an act of kindness. Three very simple things that are at the very core and basis of our faith. Many of you already do all of those things and more. But some of us do not. If not, why not? Financial responsibility, personal worship and the living out of our faith in the grace and love of Christ every day! That is what I mean when we build with balance. It was Ruston who said, "Every duty we omit obscures some truth we might have known." You see I believe that revelation comes after action. As we do what we know to do then we get further revelation about what God wants us to do. When we do what God told us to do yesterday, then today we find fresh and new answers to our prayers. Revelation follows action. We build with balance and that builds a solid life. A life that last because we all need it! You see, God is in this and we are in this with God for the long haul. It is a journey. Many think it is a process. I have to agree. It is a process by which we grow each and every day in the love and spirit and more and more in the statue and image of Christ. Because if the storms haven't hit you; they will. They will! If by some chance you have been immune to all the storms and harsh realities and difficulties, problems and troubles of life and they haven't hit you; they will. Just like the parable the storms come on both the one who builds his house on the sand and the one who builds his house upon the rock.

John Killinger tells the story of the gunner of the B-17 bomber of World War II. The gunner was in the nose of the plane. They were descending and he could see there was a huge ditch in the front of the landing strip. He knew for them it would be curtains. He tried to catch the pilots on the intercom. Finally when he got through the pilot was saying this over and over. "God, please help me not to panic. God, please help me not to panic! God, please help me not to panic!" And he didn't! What he was actually able to do, miracle that it was, was to land the plane hard on its belly right in front of the ditch and it actually bounced over the ditch onto the landing area and the plane was safe. When we build a life that last we don't panic when the storms come because we know the foundation upon which our life is built is secure. It is lasting.

This past week many in America grieved over the death of Mattie Stepanek. If you watched Good Morning at least two different mornings you heard them talk about his death. This thirteen year old little boy who had advanced muscular dystrophy, I think, died a life all too early. He wrote a series of poems called *Heartsongs*. He touched! This little boy had a big influence. This little person had a BIG life. We all wish for that kind of life. One of the things that little Mattie said over and over and over again is that you have to play after the storm. When you build a life that lasts, there is a balance and solidarity in our lives that enables us to play even after the storm has struck and is over because we know the house we are building is secure for this life and the life to come.

Gonna Lay down My Burdens
Matthew 11:16-19, 25-30

Gonna lay my burdens down! I had the privilege of hearing Asbury Jones, a young African American, preach at the Harvard Chapel during Black History Month. It was a powerful message built around a text from Scripture and a text from an old Negro spiritual. The sermon was about the sorrow and suffering of this life, but there's coming a better day. It was intellectually stimulating and emotionally moving, and moved with such power to a crescendo with that rhythmic cadence.

He said something like, "In this life we have to contend with the sorrow and suffering some more! In this life we have to contend with the sadness and the slavery some more! In this life we have to contend with the tears and the fears some more! In this life we have to contend with the disappointment and death some more, but there's coming a better day There's coming another day!"

"There's coming a day when we're gonna be on the other side, and on the other side we will contend with the sorrow and the suffering no more! We will contend with the sadness and the slavery no more. We will contend with the tears and the fears no more. We will contend with the disappointment and death no more. On that day we're gonna walk with Jesus and we're gonna talk with Jesus, and Jesus, Himself, will wipe away every tear from our eyes. We're gonna lay down our burdens, to pick them up again no more!"

Every now and then we need to hear that. Sometimes we skirt around eschatology. We do not want to be identified with those who preach only "a pie in the sky," but every now and then we need to hear that there is coming a day when no more will we contend with the sorrow and the suffering and the sadness and the slavery and the tears and the fears and the disappointment in death. We need to hear that.

But perhaps we need to hear a word of what to do in the meantime. What do we do while we are still contending with everyday life? How do we contend in our day with stress and worry and concern and lifestyles that demand something from us almost every single moment? Rest - recreation - priorities -direction, simplicity, backing off a moment, looking at what God wants to give to us when we are tired and weary and need His rest - that is what Sabbath and Service is all about.

Jesus needed a vacation; read verse 16-19. We see a side of Jesus that we have not paid much attention to. Jesus was tired. He was burdened. He said, "We played the music of celebration and you would not dance, we played the music of the funeral dirge and you would not mourn." "What do you want?" Jesus asked. Jesus was burdened by burdens placed upon Him by people who were always demanding something. Jesus needed a vacation from people that very possibly had already made up their minds to be negative and critical and cynical and basically unhappy. There are people like that. I am like that more often than I want to admit and perhaps you are like that at one time or another.

Karen Horney, a great psychiatrist, says that a psychotic is one who says two plus two equals five and is out of touch with reality. A neurotic is one who says two plus two equals four, but I don't like it. Sometimes we are like that. We just don't like the way things are. We're just unhappy, and we're gonna stay that way.

Winston Churchill told the story of a family who was picnicking by a lake, and one of their younger children fell into the water. A passerby saw what was happening, stopped, got out of his automobile, ran, fully clothed, dived into the lake and rescued the child. The mother, standing on the side of the lake the entire time, looked around and said, 'Where's Johnny's cap?' Evidently his cap had fallen off in the water. Her response to all that had happened was, "Where's Johnny's cap?"

Some folks have made up their minds that they are not going to be happy no matter what. What makes folks like that? Is it because they are dissatisfied about themselves? Is it because they do not feel good about themselves? Is it because they do not love themselves? Is it because they are not happy with the way they look or with what they have done or not done with their life? When we are unhappy with ourselves, we are unhappy with everyone and everything.

We're like Charlie Brown that says to Linus "You know from day one all I have received is criticism. From the very first moment I set foot on the stage of life they decided I was not right for the part." Sometimes we feel that we are just half a step behind and we're not right for the part. We just don't fit in. We just don't feel good about ourselves.

Dag Hammarskjold said, "A man that is at war with himself is at war with everyone around him." Perhaps we have decided to be unhappy because we are basically unhappy with ourselves. Maybe we feel that way more when we are tired. Tired is a theological category, you know. We are different people when we are tired, our resistance is low and our resources are not as vast.

Jesus needed rest and so do we. Jesus could have copped out. Jesus could have used excuses. Jesus could have walked out and said, "I'm tired of this. They don't care. No matter what I do I can't satisfy them." But Jesus did not do that. Instead Jesus says in verses 25-30, "Come unto me when you are weary and burdened and I will give you my rest." "You can't fight life on your own." Jesus says, "You can't conquer those demons by yourself, come unto me. You don't have the strength and resources, come unto me! That problem is too big, life is too big for you, come unto me! Come unto me! I will give you rest."

Now listen to me closely. Jesus is not saying that you are about to board a ship with Robin Leach and go to the lifestyles of the rich and famous. Jesus is not promising a "get away from it all" that ignores responsibility and lessens our dignity as persons. No. The opposite! Jesus' prescription for us when we are tired is to take on His burden, cooperate with Him in His work and be a part of what God is doing in the world today; see a need and meet it, see a hurt and heal it. Jesus is calling us to be a part of His great mission in the world. Jesus is calling us to be a part of a work that is invigorating, energizing and a work that means something. Most of us are not tired because our resources are exhausted.

Most of us are tired because we don't think what we're doing means anything. Jesus says, "Come unto the most exciting lifestyle that has ever been! Come unto the work that is not only here but eternal in its scope. Come unto me and I will give you a job that will wear you out but you will love every minute of it. Come unto me and I will give you my rest." "Bear my burdens," Jesus said, "do my work, cooperate with me, it is a work that will stretch you, push you, prod you and challenge the very best that is within you.

In his book, *A Room Called Remember*, Frederick Buechner has a sermon entitled "Deliverance," and it has this wonderful line, "The staleness, the sadness, the servitude of never being more than we've always been." We are called to a life that stretches and prods and challenges and moves us to be the very best that we can be. We are called to be a part of what God is doing in the world and as the old song says, "Lord, make me a captive and then I shall be free." We find rest when we find rest in Him.

We find meaning in work when we find His work to do. And we ask, "How in the world can that be restful?" "Preacher, don't tell me I've got to do more.

I can't do what I'm doing." Jesus is saying, "You carry my burden, do my work, be my child, walk and talk with me and I'll carry you."

David Livingston stood before a group in the latter part of his ministry, his body showing the effects of many years on the mission field, one arm hanging limp at his side, and talked for an hour to a group about the time he spent on the mission field. He told of almost starving to death, of almost dying from thirst several times, contacting diseases with high fevers, and the times he had been attacked by wild beasts. After the talk someone came to him and said, "Oh, Dr. Livingston, I could not help but feel so sorry for you as you told about all that you did for the Lord.' He said, "Oh please, dear madam, if I have given you the wrong impression I apologize. If I have left the wrong feeling with you, I apologize completely. For you see, I was having the time of my life" IT'S THE BEST TIRED YOU WILL EVER KNOW!

Rush to Judgment?
Matthew 13: 24-30

That was true of me when I was in the fourth grade: I volunteered to head up a little effort to enlist boys in our class to be members of Mrs. Thomas' fourth grade basketball team. I circulated a list; people came by and signed up. The last person to sign on that list was an individual that sat in the back of the class, never said anything to anyone at any time. He was very shy. He was the very last one to write his name. It was with a pencil that had not been sharpened and was almost impossible to read. I did not even turn his name into Mrs. Thomas. We had our first practice and he was there. His name was James Whitaker. At the end of the season we were the undefeated city champions because of James Whitaker. In 1964, at the state tournament, listed among the top five basketball players in the state of Alabama was James Whitaker. Not bad for a forward who stood only five foot nine and could barely write his name.

Have you ever noticed things are not always the way that they seem? It is sometimes hard to judge a book by its cover. It is sometimes hard to get a true picture of an individual or a situation by just some kind of outward view, In fact, Jesus is trying to tell us, I think, in this parable that it is very, very difficult to make judgments of that kind. Jesus told a parable which you have heard about an owner who sowed good seed in his field. Yet, while he was asleep the enemy came and sowed bad seed and when the seeds came up the weeds and the wheat came up together. The servant said, "Who did this?" The owner said, "An enemy." "Shall we cull them out?" He said, "No! Use your patience, Let them co-exist. Let them go side by side because at the end I, as the owner will execute my judgment as to when to harvest and as to how it will be carried out." An interesting note by our Lord and one of the truths is that it is very, very difficult to make those kinds of judgments.

Things are not always as they seem and sometimes they don't turn out as we expect them to. It was seen in 1874 as the answer to a lot of America's problems, like problems with hay and problems with erosion. In 1874 at the Philadelphia Centennial Expedition there on the Japanese Pavilion was this marvelous, rapidly growing plant. Its benefits were widely advertised so much so that it became the darling of the Soil Conservation Society in the United States. From 1935 to 1942 the Soil Conservation Society of the United States put out eighty four million seedlings of the plant that ate the South, and you know what it is - it is kudzu. They said it would be so beneficial. It can grow two feet in a day and it can grow fifty feet in length. If you don't believe it, come to my house and I will show you some of it. There is plenty of it. More than you will want to see. But that is Rapid growth of kudzu is exactly what caused the problem because they said it began to fowl up the hay bailers. It began to consume fields, to consume orchards. It consumed trees. It consumed houses. It consumed everything. Some say it even caused trains to slide off the railroad track. In 1943 there were twenty thousand people who belonged to the kudzu society. They even had kudzu balls. But then to its dismay and even embarrassment, the Soil Conservation Society had to change its mind and say the kudzu was now classified as a weed, because "it did more harm than good." There is a name for things that do more harm than good. There is a name for people who do more harm than good, we call that evil.

There is evil in our world today. Probably the most characteristic cartoon that I have seen in a long time was one I saw recently where children were lined to up to speak to Santa Clause after they had passed through a metal detector, Read your newspapers! This past week three officers of the law went to serve a warrant; doing what they are paid to do in Ensley, Alabama and were shot dead. One was about ready to retire. Innocent people are taken as hostages of war as political prisoners and are beheaded. We are in war today and sometimes it is hard to tell the difference between the good guys and the bad guys. Which are the wheat and which are the weeds? It is difficult to tell. From whose perspective is one a terrorist or a freedom fighter defending freedom or in loosing from bondage. I don't know that I can always tell. I don't know if anyone can always tell. That is what the judge is saying. That is what Jesus is saying. He says that sometimes we have to let them stand alone. We have to exercise patience. Now, Jesus is not saying that there are not times that we should not stand up for what we believe. Just the opposite! Jesus did that many times. Many parables speak of that.

This parable is speaking about something else. It is saying that we should stand up sometimes, Sorta like the widow, who lived somewhere near Atlanta, who was in Sherman's way on his march to the sea. When Sherman, himself, came up to her house and her farm because she refused to leave she stood on the front porch with a broom and he laughed at her and said, "Ma'am, do you expect to win this war with your broom." She said, "No, sir, but I want you to know whose side I am on." Sometimes we just have to let people know whose side we are on and then there are times, as Jesus said, that we have to be patient. Sometimes it is very difficult to make those judgment calls. In fact, sometimes it is impossible.

Our own Bill Parker tells the story of several years ago when a group of motorcycle riders came to our city on their ride with the Trail of Tears. He was sitting at a table when all of a sudden in they come with their black leather britches and black leather jackets. Their hogs and Harleys were tied outside. In they walked with their biker babes all around them and as they came in an awesome presence and eerie silence settled over the restaurant. The waitress was even a little bit nervous as she came and took their order. In fact, everybody in the entire restaurant was nervous, grinning and watching them out of the corner of their eyes. They were nervous and apprehensive until all of the bikers and their babes held hands and asked the blessing. Sometimes it is just hard to tell. Things are not always what they seem! It is difficult and sometimes impossible to make those kinds of judgments about people, but we continue to try. Oh, how we continue to try!

Most often we try to judge people because we are jealous of them. We perceive that they may have a little bit more than we have and we feel very uncomfortable about that and we question the way that they got what they have. We feel jealous and sometimes we look down upon people and think that we like to compare ourselves favorably with them. Of course, sometimes we simply judge because we are just trying to feel better about ourselves. Because we usually condemn in other people that which we see at fault in us. I am usually most vocal about the sins of others when I see that sin in myself Sometimes it is just difficult to tell between the wheat and the weeds - the good guys and the bad guys. It is just difficult to make those kinds of judgments. Probably the poet said it best when he said, "For there is so much good in the worst of us and so much bad in the best of us that it should behoove any of us to talk about the rest of us." Or as the man said, "For better to judge for we are sinners all." It is just difficult! Sometimes it is just plain impossible to make those kinds of judgments particularly when we look at Matthew's audience. It is not necessarily the audience to which Jesus spoke the parable, but the audience to which Matthew wrote the parable because that audience is the church. The Bible is clear about that. The field in which the weeds and good grain is sown in Matthew is the church.

There are good guys and there are bad guys in the church. Yes, Virginia there are hypocrites in the church. I don't know of a better place for hypocrites to be, but they are there. Why? Because sometimes I am one! Sometimes I am a good guy. Sometimes I am a bad guy. Sometimes I don't know whether I am trying to do my will or the Lord's will. Sometimes the good that I do, I don't find myself doing and that which I don't want to do, I find myself doing. I think Paul said something about that in Romans. It is just difficult to make those kinds of judgments because the church itself has a horrendous history in trying to make those kinds of judgments. Look at the crusades. Look at the inquisitions.

It was a terrible and horrendous history in trying to do God's work of judgment. Jesus said, "Don't pull it up. Because in doing so you may lose some of the faithful themselves. You may lose some good folks." Jesus said, "Let them co-exist. Use a little patience and leave the judgment to me." For you see, judgment belongs to God. Remember the success of the church does not depend upon an ethically, morally or creedally perfect people. If it does the church will always be a failure. The success of the church depends on how we show forth and live out the spirit of Christ. Imperfect sinners all are we. Judgment is God's business. Service is ours. Reflecting Christ is ours. Loving like Jesus loved is ours. Forgiving like Jesus forgives is ours. That is our business even though we might have to rub elbows, even sometimes in the church, with people who are better or less than we are.

Have you ever noticed that sometimes things are just not what they always seem? The preacher told the story of when his church was undergoing an addition. They were building an educational wing and he was proud of what the church was doing. Sometimes after the laborers had left he would wander through the buildings. One day he was in a particular part of one of the buildings that he had never been in before and was looking around late in the afternoon. He walked into a room and the door sorta swung to. He went to open the door and there was no handle on it. He was in a dark room. He did not know where he was and began to panic. He told himself to be still and quiet and let his eyes adjust to the darkness and they did. As they did he noticed standing right beside him was another person. There was a man standing there. Out of the corner of his eye and in his apprehension he saw that the man looked very large, much bigger than he. In fact he looked sorta mean and menacing. In fact, he might even characterize that man at least from first appearances as a bad or evil person. He finally said, "Sir, may I help you?" Which at that time meant what are you doing here. The man did not reply. The preachers apprehension rose and rose and he finally asked, "What are you doing here?" The man answered did not reply. Then finally the third time he reached out to touch him and said, "What are you doing here?" And in doing so he touched this menacing evil figure. He touched a mirror! The person with whom he was about to do battle was himself.

The Trouble with Evil
Matthew 13:24-30

The little country church was having its regular monthly business meeting, and the auditorium was packed in itself indicative that something important was about to happen. Now we will have the report of our Membership Committee given by Brother Jones." "Brother Moderator, if it is all right with you, I would like to consider the application for membership of Mr. Black separately from the others because he is the first of his race, the Negro race, to present himself for membership in our church. I would like to make a motion that we accept his application, and then I would like to speak to the motion."

After a few moments of speaking to the motion, another arose and said, "I would like to speak against this application for membership. After speaking a few moments, in vehement breath a voice was heard to say, "...and if he is accepted into our church, I am afraid I will have to leave; and I know others who will as well!" With that he sat down.

A vote was taken. It was 107 FOR accepting the application and 32 AGAINST. When the vote was announced, some applauded slightly and twenty-two others got up and left the little country church, the New Harmony Baptist Church.

Was that a good decision? Was, that a right decision? Was that a decision made well? What do you think?

He is leaving to go on a date. "Mom, I'll be back after a while - I'm going on a date." "Remember, Son, curfew is 11:30." "Aw, Mom!" "11:30!" At 11:30 he is nowhere to be found. At 12:30 she is still up, and he is not there. 1:30 rolls around, and finally at 2:15 the car pulls into the driveway. He comes into the house, his mother is still awake, and he says, "Oh, Mom, I am so sorry. We were having such a good time. I know I should have called." She answered, "Yes, you should have; I have been worried. What am I going to do with you? You are almost three hours late. You are grounded for two weeks."

"Grounded? I'm seventeen years old! You can't ground me! Besides, the concert is next week, and it is something I have looked forward to for months and months!" "You're grounded for two weeks."

"You just don't love me, Mother! You don't care about me anymore. I can't believe you are doing this to me! If Dad were still alive....."

Was that a right decision? Was that a good decision? What do you think?

The General is in his tent of strategy. He has just received the most disturbing news. Not only has he lost the last battle, but he has learned from a very reliable source that one of his top five aides is a spy! One is leaking information to the enemy, and that was the reason they lost the last battle! What does he do? Five aides he has trusted: four are good and one is bad. What does he do? He could fire all five of them, but then he would lose four good to find one bad. So he decides to wait, to wait and do nothing, to wait and let time weed out the evil one.

Was that a good decision? Was that a right decision or a wrong one? What do you think?

You see, the trouble with evil is that sometimes it is hard to tell the good from the bad, it is hard to tell the right from the wrong. This is especially true when we think about dealing with and making judgments about people. How nice it would be if all the good guys wore white hats, and all the bad guys wore black hats! Then we could make clear-cut decisions based on a clear identity. Of course, it doesn't work that way. Of course, some appear to be good but yet are not. There are those who seem to be shadowy, yet their motives are good. How do you tell the difference? How do we know one from the other? There are those who talk a good game but do something else, and Jesus called those people "false prophets." In spite of the ambiguity, the confusion about the good buys and bad guys, sometimes we are called upon to make decisions and to make them now.

It is the regular monthly business meeting, and it is time to take a vote. It is 2: 15 AM, and he is late; and it is time to make a decision. Sometimes in the confusion and ambiguity of the moment we are called upon to make a decision.

This past week I was walking across the parking lot of Memorial Hospital when a fellow minister stopped me. It was on Tuesday. He said, "I see you did not go to Nashville today." I answered, "No, I don't think my blood pressure could stand it." He said, "What are we going to do?" I said, "I really don't know. I think we have some difficult decisions to make some choices to be decided.

He said, "That is true, but there don't seem to be any good choices." I said, "That is right, but sometimes we have to make a decision, make a choice, and then make it good! With that he grinned. As he pulled away from me in the parking lot, he said, "Yeah!"

Sometimes we are called upon to make a decision. In the confusion and ambiguity and immediacy of the moment we are called upon to make a decision. Then we are called on to cradle that decision, nurture that decision, and make that decision a good one. We have to take a stand, we have to make a commitment and live with it. Besides, if everything were clear-cut, cut and dried; if everything were black and white, where would be the need of faith? Wherein would be the need to trust God, to let go, to believe that He will be there to take our hands if it is a good decision and to catch us if it's a bad one. Where is the need of faith if everything is cut and dried and operates according to some kind of heavenly blueprint? Wherein would be the need of faith? Besides if we wait until everything is cut and dried, black and white, right and wrong, clear and distinguished, we will never do anything! We will become stalemated, stalled; and then we will dry up on the waterless and neglected vine of indecision.

Sometimes we simply have to make a choice. We have to choose! We have to make a commitment and then make that decision a good one. Even though sometimes it may seem only the lesser of two evils. We have to make it become less and less and less evil and more and more and more good.

It is Wednesday night business meeting, and the vote is being cast. It is 2:15 AM, and the son is late; and an action needs to be taken. However, there are other times when we must wait patiently, prayerfully, and let God's will come into play and let God's harvest be gathered. That is the point of the parable that Jesus addressed Himself to in the Parable of the Tares. He said that a good man went to sow seed, and it was good seed. While the man was not looking and was asleep at night, the enemy, the Adversary, the One who is working against us in this good world, the Evil One comes in and sows bad seed.

The good seed, Jesus says later in the chapter, are the children of the kingdom, the Christians, you and me. He is not talking about the Word of God here; He is talking about people who have incarnated that word and are living in the world today. Those are the good seeds! Those are the good ones. Yet the Evil One plants bad seed, and then they begin to grow together. Then those who would harvest the seed said, "Come and look. The weeds are mixed with the wheat." The word Jesus uses is the word, *darnell*, which was a type of weed. It was slightly poisonous in Jesus day and looked exactly like wheat. It was called "bearded wheat." Only a keen and discerning eye could tell the weed from the wheat. What would you have us do?" they asked. "Would you have us go out there and remove the weeds?" The master says, "No, because if you do that at this stage, you will dislodge both good and bad seed. We will let them grow together and then at a point in the future, I will make the distinction and the harvest will be mine. The bad will be thrown away, and the good will be retained.

How do you live in a world where we have to co-exist with the seeds of the Evil One? How do we live in a world, trying to be good while living in a world that is trying to be bad? How do good and evil co-exist? How do we, who are trying to incarnate good, live with those who are sowing seeds of trouble?

I think the parable is talking to us in several words. One of those words might be this: We should not be quick to make judgments about other people, not too quick to form opinions or character assessments of other individuals. Because we just might be wrong. We might not have enough material to form a character judgment. We might not be able to form a correct one, so forming none at all is better than forming a bad one.

Let's just exclude them!" "I 'don't think we ought to let them in. They don't believe the same thing I do. "Their color is not the same as my color." "Their sex is not the same as my sex." "Their economic attainment is not the same as mine, so I think we ought not to let them in." Then God comes back and says, "Where is it written that your color or your sex or your belief or your economic attainment is normative for everyone? Where does it say that IS necessary for entrance and inclusion?"

I think He is warning us here not to be quick to exclude. "I think we should drop them from the roll. They haven't been here in seven or eight weeks!" Then Jesus comes back and says, "If you do that, who will care for them? Who will care for them if we drop them?"

"I don't think we should go to that church! You know, there are hypocrites and sinners in that church! I know some of those people and leaders, I know some of the ministers; and they are no better than I am. I don't think we ought to go to that church because there are hypocrites and sinners there." Then God says, "If I clear out all the sinners and hypocrites in the church, who will be left?"

You remember Daniel Defoe's *Robinson Crusoe* when Friday comes to Crusoe and says, If God is so much stronger than the devil, "Why doesn't He just destroy the devil?" Crusoe says, "I guess it is the same reason he does not destroy us when we sin."

The Parable is warning us not to be too quick to pronounce judgment on others about whom we do not have all the evidence, for God says, "I don't do that! That is MY business! I will do that and take care of that in my time, so you let it ride." Does that mean we sit by and do nothing? Does that mean that we sit by and become victims of everything that people would throw at us? We just silently, passively, milk-toast-like sit and absorb it all? Become victims? Develop victim mentality? Rejoice in our state of being a victim and in some kind of masochistic way even begin to enjoy it? Of course not! That is never the way of God, and it is never the way of God's people.

No, He gives us something to do, something very important. The wheat must always maintain the nature of wheat. The wheat can never become the *darnell*. The wheat can never become the weed. If it is, it is untrue to its nature. We as Christians must maintain our Christian nature and treat kindly any and all other people. We treat them with love, we treat them with compassion, even those who may not love us or like us. Even those whom we do not like! Why? Because what is the opposite? An eye for an eye and a tooth for a tooth. "An eye for an eye produces one thing: blindness! "A tooth for a tooth" produces one thing: toothlessness! It is like trying to fight fire with fire -- it doesn't work! It is like taking someone whose body is riddled with cancer and in order to fight the disease, inject cancer cells! No! The pattern of retaliation and vengeance and hatred has to be broken somewhere. There has to become an interruption of the cycle of the world which continually moves in that kind of cycle of hatred, revenge, and retaliation. Jesus says that we, the children of the kingdom, His people living in His spirit and living by His name and according to His Word, are the ones who are to be the interruption. We are the ones who are to break the cycle, and we do that by overcoming evil with good.

We overcome evil with good. When good is true to its nature, it is stronger than any evil, any power that evil can present, so He says. They come to you and slap you on the cheek. What do you do? You turn the other cheek. If they come to you with a weary, haggard look and a heavy pack and say, "Hey, Jew boy, take my pack a mile." What do you do? You take the pack a mile and then you take the "pack another mile." If they come to you and bring you into the courts and say, "I want your coat," what do you do?" You give them your shirt as well.

"If you come to the altar to bring your gift, and your brother has aught against you..." "Now wait a minute, Jesus, surely you mean 'if you have aught against your brother.'" No, He didn't say that! He said, "If your brother has aught against you, you go to your brother before you present your gift to the altar." YOU take the initiative! You take control of your life! You take a stand for what-is good-and what is right. YOU act in a loving and kind way. You don't have to be a victim and sit and take it. You can act in a loving and kind way, taking the initiative, doing what ;s right, staying true to your nature of the good seed, knowing in due time the harvest belongs to God!

Some of you may feel like victims here today, and some of you are! You are victims of sickness and disease, of the aging process, of a society that overtaxes you and then neglects you. There are some here today who are victims of cruelty within your own homes. Some of you are victims of unfairness in the world that gave you an unfair approach and an unfair set of resources with which to fight the world. Some are victims of hostility, some are victims of exclusion, some are victims of hatred. Some are victims simply because other people do not like them because of the color of their skin, their race, their belief, economic status. Some are true victims, and in some ways, I suppose all of us are victims. But we don't have to take it. We don't have to be the victim. We can choose to respond with initiative and control and overcome evil with good!

James Agee wrote a book entitled *Now Let Us Praise Famous Men*. In that book he tells the story of an experience he had working in a saw mill. He worked in a saw mill in the mid 1930's, and one of the characters in that mill with him was a middle aged African American man. Most of his responsibilities were to take care of the mules, and he probably received the same pay as did the mules! But there was one distinction in his life because four times a day, he pulled the wire. In the early morning, before the noon hour, after the noon hour, and at quitting time, he pulled the wire.

He pulled the wire that sounded the whistle that called them to work, called them to lunch, called them back to work and then called them to go home. To him when that time came, he would approach the wire take out a cheap, dollar pocket watch attached to his overalls by a greasy string, and when the clock struck the moment, he pulled the wire! And everyone else went on his timetable and acted according to when he pulled the wire.

It was that simple act of dignity, that simple act of authority and power that allowed him to go home in the evening to sit at the head of his own table and command the respect and honor of his sons. He was a victim, of course he was! But he refused to be a victim!

Some of you are victims here today. Jesus was a victim, was He not? After all, didn't they take Him away from the Garden? Didn't they take off His clothes? Didn't they take Him and beat Him? Didn't they take Him and spit on Him? Didn't they take Him and nail Him to an ugly cross? Didn't they take Him and humiliate Him?

Didn't they take His life?? No! No! No! A thousand times no! They took nothing! They did not take His life; He gave it! --. He gave it!!!

And the Winner Is
Matthew 13:24-30

There is a definite connection and inseparable union between the interpretation of Scripture and the proclamation of Scripture. The art of biblical interpretation is called hermeneutics. The art of biblical preaching is called homiletics. There is an inseparable union between what the Bible meant then and what the Bible means today. Biblical preaching is more than just taking passages of Scripture, reading them aloud and then teaching whatever you wish. Biblical preaching is more than just memorizing and quoting a lot of Scripture, as helpful as that may be. Biblical preaching takes the Scripture in its original context of what it meant then and applies what it means today. There are at least three audiences to whom this Scripture was given. The first audience was the audience that Jesus had when He originally told the parable. As you know, there was a group gathered around when Jesus told this parable. It was told at a particular place, at a particular time and to a particular group appropriate to needs in their lives. That's the first audience" Jesus' audience. About forty or fifty years later, Matthew had an audience as well. Matthew gathered this material together and put it in the form that we now have and sent it to a New Testament church. Matthew included materials that would be appropriate to the needs in their lives. Luke tells us that some materials he used and some materials he did not use. So if Luke did that, we know also that Mark, Matthew and John did so as well. Only Matthew tells this parable. It is not included in any of the other gospels. Why? Because Matthew felt under the guidance of the Holy Spirit that it was appropriate to use Jesus' words here in connection with the audience to which it was being sent. Matthew was a great preacher. So that was the second audience. The third audience is assembled here at First Cumberland Church today. I want to take what Jesus said, what Matthew collected and what the Holy Spirit inspires and apply it to our lives today.

Let me tell you what I think the Scripture says. To Jesus' audience, I think Jesus meant that the enemy is from without. To Matthew's audience, I think it means that the enemy is from within. To us I think it means that we can face any enemy with confidence because God wins. Jesus said, "The kingdom of Heaven is like a man who sowed seeds in his field, but while everyone was sleeping the enemy came and sowed seeds among the wheat and went away. When the wheat sprouted and formed heads, the weeds also appeared. The owner's servants came to him and said, 'Sir, didn't you sow good seed? Well, where did the weeds come from?" And Jesus said, "An enemy has done this." There is an opposing force out there. There is another team on the field, and you can call it whatever you wish. You can call it the wrath of God, the power of the demonic or Satan. You can call it sin. You can call it the natural results of poor choices that we make, or you can call it the random consequences of an unfinished universe. There is an opposing force to what God is trying to accomplish in our world.

This past week, which got more coverage in the media: the outstanding accomplishment of Cal Ripkin, Jr. or the O. J. Simpson trial? There's another force out there; and when you start doing good, you will find it. I guarantee it! If you begin to love indiscriminately, you will soon face that other force. You might find it in the form of vested interest, of prejudices or in the form of trying to buck the system. In the Book of Acts Paul heals a young lady from demonic possession, and they throw him into prison. Stephen, the young deacon, began preaching that God loves everyone; and they stoned him to death. Jesus, our Lord, went out doing good and they murdered him. The most dangerous person in the world is a person who loves everyone and seeks to love indiscriminately, and that person very soon will realize that there is another force out there. So, Jesus is saying: When you go out and sow the seeds of God's love. There will be another force opposing you. The enemy is from without. Forty or fifty years later, around 80 or 90 AD, Matthew collected this parable; and I think the parable can be applied in another direction of where the enemy is from within. Look again. 'Sir, didn't you sow good seed in your field? Well, where did the weeds come from?" "An enemy did this.' The servants then came and said, "Oh, you want us to go and pull them up?" Jesus said, "No! Don't do that. If you pull up the weeds in my garden, you might pull up some wheat as well." Don't run out there making premature judgments, pulling up bad weeds when you might pull up some good wheat. Just let it grow. Let the harvest come to fruition and then God will make the determination." The emphasis is different here. The emphasis is not on the enemy from without, but the enemy from within. It can be within the church. Now I know this is going to shock you, and you probably will not believe this, but there are some Christians in the church who are not perfect. It's true. There are some churches that are not perfect. The reason I know that this church is not perfect is because I'm a member. So, we might say that we have met the enemy and "they" is us. Let us think about how we will respond to evil. We will all face evil. If you haven't, you will. One way to respond to evil is to retaliate" an eye for an eye and a tooth for a tooth. Give them a dose of their own medicine and fight fire with fire. Get even. Strike back. Sometimes we are tempted to do that, but it doesn't accomplish anything. As Martin Luther King, Jr. said, "If we all took an eye for an eye and a tooth for a tooth, we would all end up blind and toothless." It just adds to the ongoing cycle of evil in the world.

How many of us are in a position to sit in judgment on anyone? I certainly am not. I don't have all the information. I make premature judgments just like the servants did. I want to go out and divide, and I don't know how to divide. Sometimes we want to exclude because we can't tell the good folks from the bad folks, and if we act too hastily, we could even pull up the wheat instead of the weeds. There is something within our churches and media today that bothers me very much, and that is a kind of Christian militarism. It manifests itself in a mean spirit and in an attitude that seeks to use unchristian methods to achieve Christian ends. I just don't think you can do that. It is a spirit that seeks to exclude and manipulate and control all in the name of Jesus. I think there is something wrong with that.

I don't think militarism and Christianity are very compatible. Retaliation is one way to respond and some have sought to respond in that way. It is hard to see our Lord advising that. Jesus told Simon Peter after Simon Peter had cut off the high priest's ear that they who live by the sword shall die by the sword, and that applies to the church as well. We could retaliate, but I find very little biblical evidence to support that. Or we could choose to become a victim. Let me be very careful here. There may be some here today who are victims of exclusion because of your faith, gender or race. There may be some here who are victims of cruelty that happened in your home. If you are a victim of exclusion, cruelty and hatred our hearts go out to you in prayerful, loving concern. Unfairness, cruelty and exclusion happens to us all, but we do not have to remain in a victim mentality.

James Agee wrote a book entitled *Now Let Us Praise Famous Men*. It is a story of a middle-aged African American man working in a sawmill In the 30's. He took care of the mules at the saw mill, and probably was paid little more than the mules were paid. Four times a day he was in charge of ringing the bell. He rang the bell for them to come to work, to stop work for lunch, to go back to work after lunch and for them to go home. Everyone operated on his schedule. He would go to the bell, take from his dirty overalls' pocket an old, cheap watch that was tied to a greasy cord; and at the appropriate time, he would ring the bell. Everyone operated on his schedule at his beckoning. That simple act of dignity and authority was what gave that man the ambition to go home and sit at the head of his table and demand the obedience and respect of his family. He was a victim, but he chose not to remain one; and we can as well. We can face any enemy that we meet with confidence, because we know and we are assured by Scripture that God loves everyone. And God is seeking with intention to love indiscriminately. There is an old fable told by the Jewish rabbis. When it came time for the Children of Israel to cross the Red Sea, God was busy; and He sent a group of angels to be in charge. As they were looking over the balcony of Heaven down upon earth, they divided the Red Sea; and the Children of Israel crossed on dry land. As the water came rushing in, destroying some of the Egyptians, the angels began to rejoice. 'We got 'em! We got 'em!" The Almighty passed by and asked, "What's going on?" "We got em! We got those Egyptians and we've freed the Israelites." And God said, "You are dismissed from my service." They asked, "Why?" And God said, "Don't you know that the Egyptians are my children too?" God loves my best friend and God loves my worst enemy every bit as much as He loves me. God loves Saddam Hussein just as much as He loves Mother Teresa. God loves Judas Iscariot just as much as He loves Simon Peter. God loves indiscriminately! God loves everyone! It is God's nature to love. God cannot help it. That is just the way God is! And we can face any enemy with confidence because we know that God loves everyone and that God is going to win. And the winner is God! One day God will make all of these judgments that we now are incapable of making. God will render a just judgment. God will balance the scales and settle all of the accounts. We might as well quit trying to do that and let God when He gets ready. That is God's business, and I am fairly assured that He will do a better job of it than I will. A movie of several years ago entitled *Stars in My Crown*, has as its central character a black man, an "Uncle Remus" type character, who lived in a small southern town on a farm. His wife had died, and he wanted to spend the rest of his days living on that farm. He had lived for many years in the community, and had befriended at least three generations of people. A precious metal was discovered right in the middle of his farm, and they wanted to start mining. So they came to him and said, "We want to buy your property." He said, "Well, if it's all right with you, I'm just not interested in selling." They said, "We have to get on. This is going to be a boom town: and we need your property." Again, "I'm just not interested in selling." Anger arose, and they began to use tactics of anger and hatred and then terror. They burned his barn. They shot into his house. Finally, they issued him an ultimatum: Either leave or we're coming after you. An old preacher friend in the town heard of what was going on and went to visit the old gentlemen. And sure enough, as night fell, here they came the leading citizens of the town in their white robes with ropes, guns and dogs. The preacher went to the front porch and said, "Well, our friend is ready to die if that is your wish, but he has asked me to read to you his Last Will and Testament. With that the preacher began to read that the old man would leave to the banker the farm which the banker had so jealously sought to have. He would leave his rifle to one of the other men standing there, who had learned to hunt using that very rifle. He would leave his fishing pole to another and to another he would leave this and to another he would leave that. And in the face of such generosity and kindness and amid such hatred those hardened men began to feel shame and walked away. Within minutes the mob evaporated. The preacher's grandson was up on a hill watching all of this. He ran down the hill and into the house, and said, "Grandpa, what kind of will was that? What kind of will did you read?" And the preacher said, "It was the will of God."

Sorting Out Wheat and Weeds
Matthew 13: 24-30

I think we all know there are good folks and bad folks; good people and bad people. I have trouble sometimes trying to distinguish between the two. Take, for example, the Jews and the Arabs. These are two groups of people, whit have historically shown a dislike for each other. Who are the good guys and who are the bad guys?

At Jesus' arrest were his best friend and his worst enemy. One was using a knife and one was kissing Jesus."

One of my dearest friends is a Jewish Rabbi who lives in Nashville. While I was doing some study in Boston, I met Yosha, an Arab, and found him be one of the most devout, religiously disciplined people I have ever known. He was a loving and caring family person; a man who had suffered injustice on his job at the hands of Christians. So, wondered are the Jews the good guys? Are the Arabs the bad guys? Or is it vice-versa? It is hard to tell sometimes.

I know there are good guys and bad guys, but sometimes it is difficult to distinguish between the two. It is sorta like when I was a seminary student serving a seminary church, and my seminary church had a basketball team in a church league. We were playing other Baptist churches. I remember one night they convinced me to play with the team. I noticed a player on the other team who was playing dirty. I mean he was just a dirty player. He fouled unnecessarily. He was always screaming at other people, showing the worst of sportsmanship. He literally was not the kind of person that you would want to play with. In fact one time I broke away for what you call a lay-up and he just literally grabbed the back of my jersey causing us both to take a tumble. I mean this was, by far, the poorest sport on the court. At halftime I asked a member of the other team, "Who is that guy, anyway?" He said, "Oh, have you not met him? Meet our new pastor."

And I wondered who the real person was: the person that got up in the pulpit on Sunday morning or the person that played basketball the way that he did? Sometimes it is hard to tell the good guys from the bad guys; the good people from the bad people. How do you do it? Do you do it by outward appearances or do you do it by a single act? Do you make that judgment on a series of acts or a lifetime of acts? How do you tell the good guys from the bad guys? Sometimes when we don't, we make things even worse.

I remember when we lived on Sea Haven Drive in Hixson, several years ago, I hated my next door neighbor. I literally hated him. He had the most beautiful yard. He was out there working in it all the time. It looked immaculate. Every single sprig of grass was exactly the same. It was awful living beside this man. So, after some persistent persuasion by my better half, I went over and asked him, "How do you do this, man? Your yard is unbelievable and mine is horrible." "Scott's turf builder." he said, "Scott's turf builder, you can't beat it." He said, "You have to get the turf builder that has weed control." He didn't tell me you are supposed to put it on in the spring. I put it on in the summer. It killed every blessed sprig of grass I had, which tells you I didn't have any grass at all. All I had was weeds. I didn't know the weeds from the grass. The turf builder did, but I didn't, sometimes it is just hard to tell the weeds from the grass. Sometimes it is difficult to ascertain who the good person is and who the bad person is.

We can get into a mess when we try to do so. I think that is somewhat of the point of what Jesus is trying to say in our parable here today. He is saying that a man came and sowed good seeds but while he was asleep, an enemy came and sowed bad seed. Then both seeds came up together. In Jesus' day the weeds he is referring to in the original language talks about *darnel* which looks exactly like wheat. So as they come up it is almost impossible to be able to distinguish between the wheat and the weed or the darnel. The servants came and asked, "What shall we do?" Jesus said that the owner said to wait until the harvest and then at the harvest time the farmer will be able to make the distinction.

What is Jesus saying here? Maybe one of the things that He is saying is that Christians and non- Christians have to coexist in the same world. Now we should avoid several extremes as we ponder this. One is that we should avoid the extreme of accepting or embracing worldly philosophies that would be unacceptable to God. Schaller says that growing churches are churches that firmly state what they believe and why they believe it. Unashamedly they say this is what we believe and this is where we stand. We must always do that! We must avoid the extreme of embracing worldly philosophy that is unbiblical or unacceptable to God.

On the other extreme, we must avoid as well trying to isolate ourselves from the world. An ivory tower Christian can never reach the world for the Lord, Jesus Christ. We have to be in the world, not a part of the world. We are to avoid the extreme of isolationism. It is the analogy of the boat. Now a boat is made to be in the water. That is the purpose of the boat - to be in the water. The problem comes if the water starts to get into the boat. It is true with the

Christian. It is our place to be in the world serving Jesus Christ and witnessing to his love. The problem comes when the world gets into the Christian. So we have to avoid the extreme of both isolationism and compromise.

We must understand that togetherness does not mean sameness. We do not have to be the same as the world but we do have to live our lives together. The difference is the living relationship that we have with the Lord, Jesus Christ. He lives in our hearts and is our relationship to the living Lord Jesus Christ that makes us different from those who have him not. So maybe he is saying at least one thing that Christians and non-Christians have to exist in the world together. Possibly he is saying in the meantime we have to wait.

The servants came and said, "Shall we dig up the weeds?" "No, if you do that you will pull up the wheat as well. You wait. Wait for the harvest." The word wait is a difficult word. But as we wait it gives us the marvelous opportunity to lay aside the terrible burden of trying to set in judgment. We don't have to make those judgments. We don't have to try to play God. We can let God be God and we can be ourselves. We can be what we are and let God take care of the rest. I don't know anyone, and especially myself, who is really capable of making those kinds of judgments. I don't have that kind of knowledge. I have partial knowledge about anyone.

I only see them at one act or one episode or one event in their life. I don't see a series of events. I don't know all of the ways of their behavior, as does God. My knowledge is very, very limited. It is limited to one time. My intelligence is very, very limited about that person and their motivation and the road along which they have traveled and where they are. I am not smart enough, and I certainly am not good enough. Because I am just like anyone else. I, too, have my faults and problems. I sometimes think what if someone were to Judge me on a single act in my history) can think of several that I am not very proud am would not want anyone to judge my entire life 0 a five-minute segment of a fifty six-year-old life.

Abraham Lincoln was right. "There is so much good m the worst of us and so much bad in the best of us it should behoove any of us not to talk about the rest of us." We are just simply not able to make that kind of judgment and when we do we usually get into trouble. It would be the same as if the servants came and tried to pull up weeds had gotten part of the wheat.

So, we try to judge prematurely or prejudge, usually get into trouble. In fact some of the greatest atrocities in the history of the humanity have been brought about by the people of God - the church. People in the name of Christ who have gone on crusades, and' witch hunts and inquisitions.

Supposedly the most Christian nation on earth before World War II, was Germany, where the Holocaust occurred. Sometimes it is just hard to tell the good guys from the bad guys. We are just incapable of doing so. So, we sorta wait until God, who is the only one capable of making judgment does so. Waiting is difficult! It is very, very difficult and demanding. We in our particular era of church history are sitting around waiting as we are in the most transitional era of Church history since the Protestant Reformation. Things are happening and people are asking "Well, is this trend or is this a fad?" Someone very recently asked me, "So, we are living in a post denomination era. Do you think the emphasis of denominations will ever return?" I say, "I don't know." People say that right now we reaching people through worship and in the past we reached people through Sunday School. Will it ever return when we will reach people through Sunday School again? I say, "I don't know." Is it a fad or is it a trend? I say, I don't know.

Brand loyalty is a thing of the past, more so outside the Bible belt than inside the Bible belt. People don't join churches anymore just because they are Baptist, Pentecostal, or Church of Christ as much as they used to. People ask me if that is a fad or a trend. I say I don't know. The most discussed topic among Christian churches today is worship. Just in the past two weeks three different churches have contacted us as they are starting contemporary or blended worship. They ask me if this is a fad or a trend. I say I don't know.

I do know this. I turn to my Bible to the fifth chapter of Acts and there I find a controversy brewing at that time in Jerusalem over Christianity and Judaism. There was a group of people, the Sanhedrin court, who felt that Christianity was not what was desired. They were about to persecute some of the early Christian leaders when a very wise man by the name of Gamaliel stood and said, "Wait a minute. If this thing is of man it is going to die off anyway. If it is of God, there is nothing in the world you can do to stop it and you might actually find yourself fighting God." How difficult it is to wait. How difficult it is to exert patience. I want patience and I want it right now:

It is difficult to wait. Maybe that is one of the things Jesus is saying. We have to wait till the end of the harvest to tell. Then we let God make the judgment because God will make the judgment. Maybe another thing that Jesus is trying to say in our parable today is that the church of God has enemies. God has enemies. Sometimes those enemies that we could call sin. We can call it making unwise decisions. We can call it Satan. We can call it the power of evil. We can call it the random consequences of an imperfect universe. But the fact is there is another team on the field. God has enemies and the kingdom of God has enemies. There are enemies out there sowing bad seeds. The only way we can tell the difference is we cannot. We let God do that! I am going to tell you something that is going to shock you, but I sincerely believe this with all my heart. Christians are not perfect. Churches are not perfect. This church is not perfect because I am a member. There is good and bad in all of us and God has enemies. Another team on the field! But yet there is coming a time. Yes, the Bible says there is coming a time of judgment when God and God alone will make that separation. Just at the end of the harvest the weeds are pulled up and tossed over here and the wheat is taken and given to the farmer, so God will make that kind of judgment. God and God alone! And that which does not belong in my life and that which does not belong in your life and that which does not belong in the church and the kingdom of God or in the world will be separated and it will be gone. Until then we are about the very awesome and sometimes aggravating task of waiting.

That wonderful old Methodist preacher, Charles Allen, used to tell the story of a farmer who wrote the editor of the papers and said, "My neighbor observes the Sabbath. He never works on Sunday. I plowed my fields on Sunday. I sowed my seed on Sunday and I harvested my crops on Sunday and I had as good or better crops than my neighbors who never worked on Sunday. Now how do you explain that?"

The editor of the paper responded succinctly and he said, "God's final accounting is not due in October..."

Be Influential
Matthew 13:31-52

I love biblical preaching, sermons with lots of Scripture, but I'm worried about this one! I think it is important for the text to be heard and developed giving structure and form to the sermon and worship service. Today you have heard a lot of Scripture. I like to use large passages of Scripture, but as I said before I'm a little bit worried about this sermon. All of you have to promise me with a solemn vow that you will never take this sermon to one of my preaching professors. Do you so promise? I think that Jim Cox and Fred Craddock would both pull out their hair, if either of them had hair, over this sermon. A sermon is supposed to have a central statement, a passage of Scripture set in its context and from that passage of Scripture a central statement. You are not going to get that today. You are going to get a series of parables strung together from which we hope to see what the kingdom of God is like. Jesus said that the kingdom of God is like.... What is the kingdom of God like?

Last Sunday we looked at a passage of Scripture which said that God is preparing us to do something, and today we are going to look at six parables that will show us what we are to do. What does it mean to be a Christian? What does it mean to live as a church member? We will see today what the kingdom of God, God's rule and reign in our hearts, is like. There are six parables and each parable is like a pearl. Each parable has its own beauty I wisdom and reflection but strung together it becomes a string of pearls and a different piece of jewelry altogether. As we look at these six parables strung together like a string of pearls and hopefully will evolve into a piece of jewelry that will allow us a glimpse of what it means to be a Christian.

What does it mean to be a Christian? What is the kingdom of God like? Jesus said the kingdom of God, if you will allow me to switch the sequence here, is like two twin parables of great discovery. A man finds a treasure in a field and he goes and sells all that he has so he can buy that field, and in joy he buys that field. Jesus tells another parable, its twin, of a merchant who is searching for pearls and once he finds that perfect pearl, goes and sells all that he has and buys it - the twin parables of discovery.

One is looking for it, another sort of stumbles upon it, but both when they find it with joy go and sell all that they have so that they might purchase it. It is what they have been looking for all of their lives. The kingdom of God comes to us in different ways. For some it comes suddenly, to some gradually, to some with a loud splash and to others very quietly. The message is: WHEN IT COMES, SEIZE IT! TAKE HOLD OF IT!

Have you ever been looking for something, couldn't find it, searching to and fro? "What are you looking for?" "Well, I can't find it..." "Well, it will be in the last place you look." "Of course, it will be." What idiot is going to keep looking for something after they have already found it? Or do we? Sometimes in our shopper's mentality to find something that is easier, quicker, better and faster, we keep searching for something we already have.

I was in a public gathering not long ago. A lady came up to me and said, "You're the pastor of First Baptist Church, aren't you?" I said, "Yes, I am." She said, "I'm a member of a church downtown but I don't go anymore." I've quit going, but I'll never move my membership. I'm going to such and such congregation. You know, all we do is praise the Lord. Isn't it wonderful?" I said, "Well, you are not going to leave your church but you like to go to this other church." She said, "I worked myself to death in my own church. I just got tired. All I have to do is go to church and praise the Lord, go home and forget it." Sometimes we search for something that is authentic when maybe what we have already is authentic.

He searched for years, looking for something he knew not what. He had an empty feeling at the pit of his stomach and a longing in his heart. He looked for it in relationships but could not be faithful in those relationships. He looked for it in other ways like drugs and gambling but never once did he find it until he was at the very edge of despair of almost taking his life. When the words "He cares for you" came to him (a verse he learned in Vacation Bible School many years before) it was in that moment he found what he had been looking for.

They tried, but could not have children. They went to every doctor they could find, and after spending great amounts of money finally started the adoption process. This process just went on and on and on. They had one meeting after another, filled out many applications and forms. They were at the point of giving up when the telephone rang. The voice on the other end said, "You've got a baby!" I ask you, could even Ted Turner buy that telephone message from that couple? When you find what you have been looking for, seize it for joy.

There is no greater joy in all of life than to find God in our hearts. The greatest, most joyful decision we ever make is when we seize the opportunity to be His child and become one of His. What are we to do? The kingdom is like the two people in the parable when they found something, they seized it for joy.

Jesus then went on to tell two other parables, twin parables, which tell about great influence. He told a parable about a mustard seed. I'm talking about a seed not much larger than the size of the head of a pin. Yet, from that small seed grows a big and beautiful tree. He talks about a piece of yeast or leaven even though it is very small. Once it penetrates the dough. It influences the entirety of the dough. Twin parables of influence. When we find God's kingdom in our hearts it then becomes our purpose and our responsibility to share that kingdom with others and to penetrate the society in which we live and tell them of the love that we know in Jesus Christ.

Our church for the past few weeks has received some marvelous publicity concerning the renovation and new buildings. The media has been wonderful. Gary Mac from Channel 12 interviewed me right in this very Sanctuary, and I was telling him about our Missions Fair, the mission and ministry of this church and the many things in which this congregation is involved right in our community in downtown Chattanooga. He said, "You know, some might criticize you and say that the church needs to stay in its walls and the church doesn't need to be out there by McDonalds or by the shoe store." Of course, I knew he was setting me up and getting me to say what I wanted to say. I said, "But yet, what better place for the church. Where should the church be if it is not by McDonald's and not by the shoe store? That is where the church is to be, in society, penetrating society with the love and grace of the Lord Jesus Christ.

How many sermons did Jesus preach in a church building? There are seventeen sermons in the Book of Acts, only two are preached in any kind of church or religious building. We are to be out there being the mustard seed and the leaven and the salt and the light that penetrates society with the love of Jesus and influencing the world for Him. That is the responsibility of every single one of us. Every one of us has a responsibility and a place to be with a role to play. We might ask, "Well, what can I do? I am just one."

Several years ago in 1975 a housewife and mother by the name of Judy Petrucci was tired of all the strip joints in her community of Lions, right outside of Chicago. She tried to do something about it but could not because no one would listen to her. Her sister came to her and said, "Judy, if you would go to law school and become a lawyer, you could put yourself in a position to do something about it and she did. She went to college, then to law school. In the meantime she ran for an office in her community. She ran in 1975 and was defeated. She ran in 1977 and was defeated; she was defeated on and on until in 1987 she was elected to the city board and then two years later she was elected as the mayor of Lions. She immediately began an Investigation of the strip joints in that area and to this very day she has been responsible for the closing of all five of those strip joints, twenty-six people have been prosecuted for tax fraud or prostitution and every one of the local officials who supported that kind of behavior' in the community has been put out of office. Property values in that community have risen twenty-five percent. One person made the difference. God has called us to be that person. We are to make a difference in the world for Christ. We are to be influential.

Jesus then follows these two parables with two other parables that just sort of weave their way in and out of our text. One is a parable about weeds and crops that grow up together and are indistinguishable except at harvest time. He tells about throwing out a fish net, good and bad fish both are caught in the same net and drawn together. Not the fisherman but the heavenly being separate the good from the bad. Well, what does that mean? What does that have to do with the rest of this parable? How does that paint a picture of what it is like to be in the kingdom of God? He is saying seize the opportunity. Make your influence known but it may not always be as tidy as we would like for it to be. The net is drawn and both good and bad come but it is God's purpose not ours, it is God's responsibility, not ours to exclude or to divide or to judge, that's God's business.

I was pastor for four years of the Indian-Kentuck Baptist Church in Canaan, Indiana. It was the second oldest Baptist church in that state, founded in 1812. They had the church minutes that went all the way back to 1812. It was a marvelous thing to read them. It was really interesting to read the minutes of the early 1800's because that congregation, like other congregations of its time, was more intent on who they could put out rather than in who they could bring in. The minutes were filled with times where they would say that a committee went and "treated" with so and so because they had done such and such. One person was actually tossed out of the church because they stole a dolly.

I read this past week of a congregation that was talking about a similar document of their church in 1860 which says that certain people were put out of the church, some for dancing and some for smoking and some for drinking and some were put out because they had been fraternizing with the Methodist. Heaven forbid. Those are extreme examples of course. It is not our place to exclude. It is our place to seize our opportunities and that's what we have been preparing to do. That's what the last three years have been about, preparing a ministry to reach out into the community and to bring in. If there needs to be any judging or separation, that's God's business, not ours. Ours is to seize the opportunity and to bring everyone in who will come.

These six parables about kingdom life and what the church is all about ends with a word to the teachers. There is no greater calling than that of a teacher. The teacher of the law who has been instructed about the kingdom of Heaven is like the owner of a house who brings out of his store house new treasures as well as old. A church tied to the past becomes involved and tangled in a rut. The church looking only toward the future loses its foundation and just can sort of flitter away into a cloud of nothingness. God's church combines the best of the past with a vision of the future and ministers today.

The church finds a balance. A delicate balance of the new and the old. The teacher is such a point of contact and sets the point of the fulcrum upon which everything else depends, nurturing the past and visioning the future, of bringing out of the store house that which is old and that which is new. That's what Gateway 2000 was all about. That's what our Missions Fair was all about. That's what today is all about. We have prepared ourselves to show a community what the Kingdom of God is like. It will be untidy, it won't be as tidy and nice and neat as we would like for it to be and sometimes it might even get a little bit messy. Almost anytime you deal with people it is going to get a little bit messy but with all the change, with all of the untidiness, there is an anchor, there is a solid foundation and that foundation is Jesus Christ.

No matter what we do today, no matter how we nurture the past of yesterday, no matter how we envision the future of tomorrow, we must always be anchored to the anchor and that is Jesus Christ. He is our anchor in the future, no matter what it may bring. He is the solid rock upon which we stand. He is the point to which we always return.

When is it Okay not to be a Christian?
Matthew 18:21-35

I believe it was Yogi Berra who said, "When you come to a fork in the road, take it!" Not long ago, I did exactly that. Sharlon and I were driving down Rossville Boulevard when I came to a fork in the road. I couldn't decide which one to take, and by the time I took one, the gentlemen driving the pickup truck behind me was almost run off the road because of the way I was driving. By the time he righted his truck and was able to pull up beside me, he shouted at the top of his voice (I'm surprised you didn't hear him), "Open your eyes, old man!" I turned to Sharlon and said, "He called me an old man!" She laughed and said something about being thankful that he didn't call me worse. I've thought a lot about that. He should forgive me for almost causing the end of his life, but how in the world am I ever going to forgive him for calling me an old man?

Sometimes forgiveness is very difficult, like when your brother-in-law calls you for the third time this year asking you to help him out with his rent, and he's calling from his cellular phone in his new BMW. Sometimes forgiveness is difficult!

Let's get to the heart of the matter. Let's talk about it from the nitty-gritty. Sometimes it is very difficult to forgive. It's difficult to forgive that fellow worker who lied about you and cheated to get a promotion and increase in salary, and you did not. How can you forgive a sibling who will not help supply funds toward the care of your parents, but scathingly criticizes everything that you do? How do you forgive a father whose demands for perfection could never be met? How do you forgive a mother who played favorites and you were not one? How do you forgive a child who uses and uses and demands and demands but never gives anything in return, not even gratitude? How do you forgive that significant adult who was entrusted by others with your care, and they abused you emotionally, physically and may even have abused you sexually? How do you forgive that ex-spouse who has taken the best years of your life and wanted to take a lot more?

How do you forgive? It is very difficult. Do you have a problem with forgiveness? Let's get right to the heart of the matter. Are there people in your life that you need to forgive and you're finding it very difficult to do so? Sometimes we all find it difficult to forgive. Apparently Matthew's audience was having a problem with forgiveness since he included this parable in his gospel, and he was the only gospel writer to do so. Simon Peter, also, was having a problem with forgiveness because he said to Jesus, "Lord, how many times are we supposed to forgive someone?" The rabbis said, "Three times." Simon Peter, trying to be a bit generous, said, "Seven." That sounded generous to Simon Peter, but Jesus said, "No! Seventy times seven." Numbers that mean unlimited forgiveness.

Jesus is saying here that the distinguishing characteristic of the Christian community and the church is forgiveness. Simon Peter is almost asking, "Well, Lord, when is it okay not to be a Christian?" And Jesus says, "Never!" It's difficult to forgive. Let me ask you another question: When we do not forgive, who are we hurting? Who are we hurting when we refuse to be Christian? Who are we hurting when we refuse to forgive? The Polynesian tribes used to hang the shrunken heads of their enemies in the front of their dwellings to remind their children whom they were to hate. Who hurts from that?

Courtney Love was interviewed this past week by Barbara Walters. Love quoted her mother who said, "Courtney, why are you going around with a hole in your chest because you had a bad childhood? Get over it!" Who is she hurting?

True story. A man bought a brand new Cadillac and it made a bumping sound that could not be found. There was a bump, bump, bump sound all the time. Finally they took off one of the doors and inside the door was a coca cola bottle and inside the bottle was a note from a factory worker that read, "Took you a long time to find it, you _____! The factory worker was resentful because he could not afford a Cadillac and resented anyone who could. Who hurts when we nurture grudges and carry around that huge bag of injustices all the time? Who gets stuck in life and cannot move on? You guessed it. We do!

Very few things are as destructive to us as unforgiveness, and that is why Jesus told this parable. In this parable Jesus is saying that sin is a very serious matter. He tells the story of a king who wanted to balance the books, so to speak. So he had a servant who owed him ten-thousand talents, an unbelievable amount of money in that day. It would take a common worker in Jesus' day one-hundred and sixty thousand years to earn that much money. We're talking about an insurmountable debt. But yet, the king forgave him. The servant got down on his knees and begged forgiveness and the king extended mercy. You would think that being extended mercy, grace and forgiveness would have caused him to be merciful and graceful and forgiving, but it did not.

The servant went out immediately and found a person who owed him about a hundred day's wages. That also was a pretty good sum of money, but not insurmountable. He grabbed him by the throat, regardless of the grace that had been extended him, and demanded that he be paid what he was owed. The fellow servant was not able to pay and asked for patience, but the first servant had him thrown into prison. Other servants heard about it and told the king. The king brought the first servant back and asked him, "Should you not have extended the mercy to him that I extended to you?" What answer did he have? None! The servant that was forgiven of the insurmountable debt was thrown into prison to pay back the original debt. The Bible takes sin seriously and the Bible takes forgiveness and unforgiveness very seriously.

Why couldn't the first servant forgive? Let me ask you a question: Why can you not forgive? Why do you find it so hard to forgive? Is it because you have never accepted God's love and grace for yourself. Is it just easier to keep our old bookkeeping method going? Is it just easier to go back to the old "this for that" and hate and revenge and resentment? Or perhaps we don't forgive because we like to control things. We're all control freaks to a certain degree. When we forgive that person that "let's loose that person, "the Bible says," and does not keep him bound to us any longer. Maybe we just want to keep things tightly under control. Or maybe it is just simply a matter of pride because to forgive someone, we have to realize that we have more in common than in difference.

We have to swallow our pride. We have to give up the false notion that we are better than they are, and admit that we are just like they are in order to be able to forgive them. Don't get me wrong -- forgiveness is not sentimentality. It's not becoming a door mat for the world to walk on. Forgiveness is not like Flo who forgives Andy Capp every: time he goes out and cheats on her, knowing he has no intention of ever changing. It's not toleration. It's not a lack of moral or ethical standards. It's not condoning sin. It's not gushiness or mushiness. Forgiveness takes sin very seriously. Forgiveness takes the sinner seriously and also the one who has been sinned against. Forgiveness takes the violation, the violator and the one violated very seriously. It's not forgetting. We can't control our memories. God can control his memory, but we cannot control ours. But sometimes to remember sin may help us to help others in the future.

What is forgiveness? When does it start? And how are we able to take the first step in trying to forgive someone? It may be when we begin to define our life by God's grace, a gift to us, rather than the hurts and injustices we feel. In a sense, forgiveness is not an act of the will; it is a by-product of our own self-cleansing. We realize that if we are ever to get on with our life, if we are ever to clean up our act, if we are ever to be whole again, we don't need grudges, hatred or resentment. When we define our lives by God's grace that has been extended to us, rather than the hurts and injustices we have suffered, we realize that everyone is a sinner, including us. We're all sinners. We've all done wrong. We all need to forgive and we all need to be forgiven. As C. S. Lewis said, "We can forgive the inexcusable in others because God forgives the inexcusable in us."

Perhaps you saw on TV this past week the story of Chris Carrier and David McCallister. Many years ago at the age of nine, Chris Carrier was kidnapped by a lone assailant. He was tortured with burning cigarettes and shot with a weapon in the head, taking out one of his eyes. He abandoned him, and he was found seven days later by a hunter.

Many years later, David McCallister was dying in a nursing home; and he admitted that he was the one who abducted, tortured and tried to kill Chris Carrier. When Chris Carrier heard that, he began visiting the nursing home every single day to show mercy, love and forgiveness. David McCallister, through dying lips said, "Chris Carrier is the greatest friend I have ever had." Do you know what the clincher was? Chris Carrier, the one who forgave, the one who had been tortured, the one who was almost killed, said, "It must have been a lot worse on him all these years than it was on me." Wow! That's forgiveness!

We are to begin to identify with them, just as Christ identified with us. We realize that we are all sinners, we're all in the same boat and we identify more with them, think more about them than we do ourselves. Can you feel how freeing and liberating and how redeeming that is?

An old Native American was converted to Christ very late in his life, and it caused a one-hundred and eighty degree change in his life. He became generous and kind and loving and merciful. Everyone was in awe of the change that had occurred in his life, and they asked him one night around the campfire, "How did this remarkable change come about?" The old Indian saw a little worm crawling in the dirt and he picked it up. Without saying a word, he held it very close to the flames of the fire and about the time the worm was to be burned, he pulled the worm away and said, "Me! The worm." We're all sinners!

In Heaven there is only one kind of person - a forgiven sinner. There are no good guys, there are no bad guys, no one has earned a place because of his integrity, holiness or good works. We're all forgiven sinners by the grace of God. In Hell there is only one kind of person - a forgiven sinner. There's only one difference. In Heaven the forgiven sinner has accepted the forgiveness that already is his through Jesus' death on the cross and becomes a channel of grace to others. In Hell the forgiven sinner rejects the forgiveness that already is his through Jesus' death on the cross and blocks that forgiveness to others.

Which are you?

Unless You Forgive
Matthew 18:21-35

His name is Kevin and every week he paid one dollar. He paid one dollar every week to a family he would rather forget. It went on for nine hundred and thirty six weeks - eighteen years, one hundred and ninety six months.

On the first Friday of 1982, Kevin was driving under the influence of alcohol and killed a young lady. She was eighteen. He was seventeen. He was sentenced to reckless driving and to manslaughter. He served the court sentence. He served one year helping to stamp out drunken driving and even though he did not have to, he continued for six more years. He was sued for one point five million dollars. They settled for nine hundred and thirty six to be paid out one dollar a week for nine hundred and thirty six weeks to the family. The problem is that Kevin forgets to pay the money. It is not that he is trying to defy the court order. He says that he has been tormented by the death of the young girl and he is tortured by the weekly reminders. Four times they have taken him to court to make him pay the dollar a week. The last time he spent thirty days in jail. Nine hundred and thirty six dollars. A dollar per week.

No one could doubt that the family had a right to be angry. No one could doubt that the family had right to feel dismayed and terribly distraught over such a tragic, tragic situation. There is no doubt whatsoever that this kind of sin, this kind of wrong must be remedied. It must be punished. There is no doubt whatsoever. You have to take that kind of act very, very, very seriously. The question remains, "How much is it right to demand? How much should be demanded?" After the nine hundred and thirty six weeks is there peace of mind? Is there freedom and release after so much remorse and restitution? Or maybe the question is better put, "How much do I demand before I will forgive?" How much do you demand before you will forgive? Every person in this room, every person on this planet has done wrong and every person has been wronged. How do we weigh that in the balances, and how do we deal with that? How much do we demand before we will be forgiven?

Jesus told a parable about that. He asked a question, "How many times should forgive?" Seven times? That is sorta what the Jewish law required. Jesus replied, "No, much more than that, seventy times seven." An unlimited number. Unlimited forgiveness. Unlimited forgiveness! Then Jesus tells the parable. It is rather an amusing parable in some ways and rather off the wall in other ways because here is a man who owed a tremendous amount of debt. He owed debt beyond our imaginings. A daily worker in Jesus' day would have to work one hundred thousand years to pay off this kind of debt if he paid every penny he earned. Someone has calculated that it is somewhere around, in our modem day terms, one point two billion dollars, an unbelievable amount of debt. His master says to his slave, "Well, pay me." "I can't." he said. "We will throw you in prison and sell your family ....." He said, "Please! Please! Please!" He forgives him and wipes the slate clean.

But then that very same servant who had been forgiven much goes out and sees another slave that owes him a smidgen amount, and demands payment. He begins to choke him. He cannot pay and is thrown in prison. When the master hears of this, he revokes his forgiveness, places the wicked servant in prison and Jesus says, "This is how your heavenly father will treat you unless you forgive." We cannot stretch the analogy here and we cannot allegorize the parable, it is a parable of contrast, not a parable of comparison. God never, ever revoked his forgiveness. Once God forgives you, He forgives you and forgets it from now on. We cannot stretch the analogy too much but still the point is made - unless we forgive.

Forgive we say. You mean I have to forgive that person who abused me as a child. You mean I have to forgive that boss who laid me off when my child was sick. You mean I have got to forgive that spouse who dumped me for a better or newer model. I have got to forgive that parent who abandoned me. You see, this sin is serious stuff. It hurts people. It ruins lives. It put scars upon us that we never outgrow and you say forgive. It seems almost cheap as we talk about it that way, but forgiveness is not cheap at all. Forgiveness is very, very serious stuff. For you see forgiving someone does not mean we forget. Reasonably, we cannot forget the wrong that has been done to us and in fact in some ways remembering that may help us to prevent it in the future. Forgiveness is not being permissive. It is not being tolerating of evil or sin. It is not being without ethical demands. Forgiving someone is not making excuses for the wrong that has been done.

Sin is serious stuff. Sin is taken very, very seriously. The debts are taken very, very seriously in Jesus' parable. It is not some milk toast, doormat, masochistic approach that we enjoy being harmed. We have to take it very seriously. But, forgiveness is an act of the will, but much more than that, it is a byproduct of when we seek our own healing. When we seek to heal ourselves and define ourselves by the love and grace that has been extended to us and not the hurt that has been inflicted upon us, we begin to define ourselves in God's image. It is a decision that we make each and every day, I think. It is a decision that we make each and every day - will we allow ourselves to be defined by that which has occurred to us and been inflicted upon us or will we allow ourselves to be defined by the grace and mercy that has been extended to us. And when we define ourselves by the mercy and grace that has been extended to us, we find that we no longer need our hatred, our anger, our resentment, our grudges because we want to be known by love, goodness and grace. For you see someone has to break the cycle when an evil is done and then retribution and then another evil is done and then retribution and then another evil is done and then vengeance and another evil, etc. Someone has to break that ugly cycle. If not, we devour ourselves and the world in its wake. Someone has to break that ugly, ugly cycle.

I once read about a tribe of Polynesians who at the doorpost had shrunken heads of their enemies to remind them of who they needed to hate. We don't want to be like that. We would not do that, but then how many times do we retain our own labels, our own grudges, our own feelings, our categorizing of entire groups of people and we keep them put down in our own thinking. We like to think we are superior to who they are. You know - "He is one of those." "She is one of those." In that we remind ourselves of who we must hate. Someone has to break that ugly cycle. Someone has to show love and grace. In *The Merchant of Venice*, Shakespeare's character, Portia, reminds Shylock that the quality of mercy is twice blessed. It blesses the one who gives it and it blesses the one who takes it. There must be inserted into that vicious cycle of hatred, impatience and bitterness; forgiveness, love and joy. There is great joy in forgiving. There is great joy in setting ourselves free and coming to our own healing, but there is also great joy in setting another free. I will not limit you by my feelings. I will not bind you by my feelings of ill will. I set you free by God's feelings of love and grace.

It is not an easy thing to forgive. We generally must stop and admit that something has happened; that a hurt has been rendered and that there are consequences and we must face it and face it quickly. Just ignoring it will not make it go away. If we have been wrong, we admit it and admit the consequences that could occur in our lives and in the lives of others. But on the road to forgiveness, we sometimes begin to and are able to, through God's strength, swallow our pride and begin to identify with the person who has wronged us. When we do so, we quickly discern that we are probably more like them than we are different from them.

The things I detest in other people are usually the things I detest in myself. On the road to forgiveness we begin to identify with that other person's situations and we find out that we are much more alike than we think. We then begin to voluntarily give up our own rights to always be right. No one owes us anything. The government doesn't owe me a thing. The church doesn't owe me a thing. Society doesn't owe me a thing. My parents don't owe me a thing. I have no right to demand that I am always treated fairly. The world is not fair and I am a part of that unfairness. I do not always treat everyone else fairly either. And then we begin to remember that while we may not be able to forget what has been done to us, we can relinquish our control over that individual. We can leave the consequences of that act to God and we do not have to bear the responsibilities for it ourselves. We do not have to seek vengeance. We do not have to seek retribution. That is God's business if it is to be its certainly not ours. Somebody might say, "Well, preacher, that sounds so easy and it sounds so unjust and unfair. Somebody needs to pay for this." When something happens like that to that magnitude - a person killed or a person mistreated or abused - somebody has got to pay. Somebody has got to pay!" He already has. Jesus has already paid for my sins and your sins and for everybody else's sins.

Robert Capon in his book, *The Parables of Judgment* talks about this wonderful parable and he says, "Everybody in the world is a forgiven sinner." Everybody in the world is a forgiven sinner. There are some forgiven sinners in heaven because they have accepted God's forgiveness and they have extended it to others. There are other forgiven sinners who are in hell because they refuse to accept it and block God's forgiveness to themselves. What a sobering thought it is. What a sobering thought it is as Jesus mentioned in the Lord's Prayer that "we are to be forgiven as we forgive others." What a sobering thought. That which I extend to others is that which will be extended to me. I have read this parable many times. I have preached on it several times and almost every time I finish the parable I tell myself that I need to be more forgiving. I mean, I am only saving my own neck. If I want to be forgiven; I have to forgive - right? Then I think what a selfish approach. I just forgive someone because I want to save my own neck. Does that in any way whatsoever resemble Jesus Christ? No! I forgive not because I am trying to save my own neck or to appear self-righteous; I forgive because God has forgiven me. I extend mercy because God has extended mercy to me. I am generous and kind because God is generous and kind to me. I am generous because God is generous and kind to me. I am gracious to others because God is gracious to me. I mean, we are only talking about our own soul.

Luther Joe Thompson served this church for many faithful years. In his book, *Lord. Help Me Make it Through the Day*, he tells the story of Jonathan Edwards. He calls Jonathan Edwards probably the finest mind of Colonial America. Very few would argue with that. Jonathan Edwards was born to a modest environment. He went to Yale and studied for the ministry and at twenty six years of age he inherited his grandfather's church at South Hampton. In five years at the ripe old age of thirty one he was famous. He was famous not only in the United States but also across the water. He was one of the greatest preachers of his generation. Ten years later everything had gone wrong. Everything had gone wrong in his church and four years later in 1750 he was fired. He was fired! The most famous preacher in the world was fired from his church, the church in which he became famous. He was fired from the church which he inherited from his grandfather. He was dismissed. He could not find work. He had a wife and ten children. The church could not find a pastor and he could not find work. So, they came to him and said, "Would you be our supply preacher until we can find someone else?" He did. I mean sometimes you just have to do what you have to do. And then sometimes you have to do what is right. Can you imagine being the supply preacher of a church that just a few months before said, "We do not want you." We are only talking about our soul.

Grumbling about Generosity
Matthew 20:1-16

It's getting dark and nervously she paces in her modest home. She is worried. Nervously, she sweeps the dirt floor from one side to the next. She stares into the darkness, it is late and she begins to pray, "O God, O God, where is my Joseph? Where is he, Lord? It is getting late and I know he didn't find work today. I went to the market place and I saw him still standing there late in the afternoon. O Lord, where is he? Has something happened to him, or is he too ashamed to come home again empty handed?"

Her prayer is broken by a tug on her dress. It's her five year old daughter Elizabeth. Little Elizabeth asks, "Mama, where is Daddy? Why has Daddy not come home yet? Is he bringing us something to eat? Mama, I'm hungry." And with that the door burst open and he says, "Hello, Elizabeth Hello, Rebecca! Prepare the table, we have a feast! Look! I have bread, I have cheese, I have figs and for the two women in my life, a little bit of honey!"

"Joseph, where did you get all of this? I know you didn't work, I went by the market place and I saw you standing there late in the day." He said, "The most amazing, the most marvelous thing happened to me today. I was standing in the market place waiting for someone to come by and hire me. The day was getting late and many had given up. Others had gone to work and just a few of us were standing there. I just couldn't come home empty handed again. I couldn't stand another night just lying in bed when sleep would not come. The growling of my empty stomach could not drown out her words, 'Daddy, I'm hungry,' and I was almost ready to give up when around the eleventh hour the most unusual thing happened. A fellow came up and he yelled to us and asked us why we weren't working. We said, "No one has hired us. He said, "I'll hire you! Come on and work!"

"It was late in the day but a few pennies was better than nothing at all, so I went and worked in the vineyard. There were people there who had been working a long time. You could tell they were tired and hot and dusty. We worked for only an hour. Then the land owner gathered us together to pay us, and would you believe he paid us first, the ones who had only worked an hour, not those who had worked three hours or six hours or nine hours or twelve hours, and would you believe he gave us wages for an entire day? We worked one single hour and we were paid for an entire day! I was so happy I was so joyously I ran to the market place and bought all of this food. Doesn't it look good? Isn't it wonderful? We shall have a feast tonight."

"As I was in the market place, I heard some of the workers who had worked longer than I had grumbling. They were just down right mad. I didn't say anything, I just came on home. I couldn't wait to get home and spread this feast before your eyes. Let us gather around table and thank God for the favor He has bestowed upon us."

"Joseph, may I ask a word?" "Yes, honey." "I'm curious, why are there just three loaves instead of the customary four? And are my eyes deceiving me, it looks like someone has cut off half of the cheese." "Well, you're right. I hope it's okay but on the way home I thought of the widow Sarah and I stopped by her house and gave her some of the bread and cheese. And wiping moisture from her eyes, Rebecca says, "Oh my dear Joseph, my kind and generous Joseph you know that it is more than alright. Let us now bow and thank God."

You may not have ever heard that parable in this way, a little different angle. It's a strange story. It really is strange when you think about it. What would the United States government do with this? What would the labor relations do with this? What would the unions do with this? What would a good attorney do with this?

Right in the middle of this is the landowner - peculiar. You know the land owner represents God and shows to us a side and angle to the nature of God. This land owner is unpredictable and generous to a fault. He will do what he will with his favor and with his money because he wishes to do so.

Why did Jesus tell this strange and unusual parable? In the 19th chapter of Matthew a man came to Jesus. He is called the rich young ruler. He came to Jesus and wanted to be Jesus' disciple. To make a long story short, Jesus said, "You will have to sell what you have and give it to the poor, and then come and follow me." The Bible says that he went away sorrowfully. He simply would not do what Jesus asked.

Jesus also says in the19th chapter that it is more difficult for a camel to go through the eye of a needle than it is for a rich man to come into Heaven, but with God all things are possible. That just blew the minds of the disciples, and they then asked who could be saved. They felt if you were rich it was because God was honoring you and if you were poor it was because God was punishing you, and if a rich man could not get there, who could?

Then Simon Peter said, "Lord, we have given up everything to follow you, and we know we've got a lot coming. Simon was trying to move himself into position, trying to scoot himself up next to Jesus so that when Jesus came into His kingdom he could get all the goodies. He was thinking how he could manipulate and control and get all of those things that comes to those who are favored by God. Peter is wanting the choice church, the honorary doctorate, a sign out front that has Reverend in front of his name that reserved parking place with his name on it, a clergy sign on the front of his automobile where he could go to the hospital and get that convenient clergy parking place, a country club membership. Peter wanted all of those perks and discounts and ministerial advantages. Jesus said that there would be rewards alright and they would be beyond our imagination but they will not be given out the way we think they are going to be given out. Strange story!

Then Jesus tells this parable about some who work one hour and got paid as much as those who worked twelve hours. Now the land owner honored his agreement with those who worked twelve hours. They got exactly what they contracted for. The land owner was generous and kind to those who only worked an hour. He didn't want them to go home empty handed to a hungry family.

Where are you in this parable? I'm sure that probably every single one of us here at some time have been the one hour worker and sometimes we have been the twelve hour worker. There are people who have done so much more than we. What kind of chance do you have in comparison to missionaries? Think of all those years in school, think of having to learn different languages, think of being away from family, think of never getting to see your kids and your grandchildren, think of being in hostile countries with all kinds of crazy diseases. What chance do we have against those kind of people?

Think of those bi-vocational ministers, many times deprived of education but faithfully week in and week out doing the very best that they can with those small congregations. They love the Lord and love the people, but never make enough money to get ahead, and when they come to the end of their life they have very little money in retirement, have probably lived in parsonages all their lives and probably don't even have a roof over their head. How do we stand a chance with people like that?

Think of that mother who single-handedly, either through death or through an uncaring husband, is raising children all by herself. She sacrifices and works and does without to see that her children get things that you and I just take for granted. How do we measure up against people like that? We don't!

Sometimes we see ourselves as the twelve hour worker. I mean we've been in it all day long, we've been in the baking hot sun and the dry and dusty heat is choking our throats. We have worked in the nursery for thirty years. We have changed more diapers than Gerber. We have done it all. We have worked in Vacation Bible School in the hot part of the day. We've listened to more dry, dusty sermons than we can count. We've tithed and every time the church would have a special program then we would give above our tithe. We've served on every committee. We have been there every time the door has opened and sometimes we have dragged our children screaming and hollering to the church. We've done it all. We've been there, we've been the pillar of the church. We sometimes feel that the church could not get along if we were not there.

Here they come, bopping in the church with their flowered short sleeve shirts and Bermuda shorts and tennis shoes and their crazy looking hair and say, "Man, let's get turned on to Jesus'" And they get turned on to Jesus. They have never listened to any of those long dry, boring sermons, never worked in Vacation Bible School. They think John 3:16 is a rest room on the third floor. They don't know a benediction from an introit. They know nothing! They respond to Jesus in faith and they are going to get the same thing we are? Wait a minute! Is this fair?

We have a choice. We can either be gracious and thankful for what God has given to us or we can gripe and complain and grumble that God has been gracious to others. Sometimes it is hard for us to celebrate God's goodness to someone else. It is difficult to be happy because God has been good to someone else and probably someone that we don't think is as deserving as are we. It is difficult when we work twelve hours in the long hot sun and we get paid the very same thing as that person who worked only one hour. It is sometimes hard to celebrate the goodness of God when it is extended to someone else.

It is easy to be bad when God is good. That's what happened to Jonah. God told Jonah to go and preach in Nineveh, and he took off the other way but God finally got him to Nineveh. He finally preached, pronounced that doom like he loved doing. But low and behold the people repented. And Jonah was as mad as an old wet hen. He said, "Lord, that's the reason I didn't want to go there. I knew they would repent. I knew you would be gracious because I know that you are a gracious and long-suffering God. Sometimes it is hard to be grateful when God is good to others when we don't think they deserve it as much as we do.

For some of us it is a personality thing. We decided a long time ago that we're going to be miserable. We sort of feast on melancholy. That is just sort of a natural state of life for us. We like it that way. It feels good to feel bad. "That's a beautiful dress you have on. . ."Oh, this old thing. It is old and faded and doesn't fit right. It's difficult to iron. I bought it at a yard sale on credit."

"Heard you had a wedding in your family." "Yea." "I know that everyone is really happy." "Well, we're waiting, you know sometimes these marriages don't work out." "Heard you had a new baby in your family. I know everyone is excited. Boy or girl?" "A little girl, named her Elizabeth." "Oh, that is wonderful!" "Well, we're not getting too excited yet. You know how some of these little girls can be. It's a personality thing. It's just part of our nature. We have a hard time being happy.

The wonderful thing is that God has come to change our nature. God has come to make us gracious. God has already done His part. God has been generous to us. He sent His Son Jesus to die on Calvary's Cross for you and for me, because of His love and His grace you can be forgiven and have a home in Heaven. Our part is to accept it and be gracious. We can't do anything else. I have never met one single person, and I have known and do know some great Christians, that had any kind of claim on God. Not one! Not by our money or our good works or anything that we can do or say have one ounce of claim upon God. It's all grace. It's all God's work of grace in us to make us gracious. We can spend the rest of our lives grumbling and envying and complaining and griping or we can live our life in gratitude and be gracious.

This is a stewardship sermon. We're not filling the air with "oughts" and "shoulds." You ought to tithe, you ought to give, you ought to support your budget, and you ought to give your time and talents to God's work. You already know that. A lack of knowledge is not the problem. It is lack of motivation. We are motivated and our nature is changed when we realize what God has done for us. There is not one single thing on God's green earth we can ever do to merit one ounce of God's favor. We have no claim on God whatsoever. None! It's all grace. Out of the heart of gracious love, God forgives us and loves us. If you could give one gift to your children, what would you give to them? Would that gift be gratitude? I have never known a thankful and gracious person who was mean spirited or manipulative. God's work of grace is to make us gracious. He has made more headway with some of us than he has with others of us. "Nothing in my hand I bring, simply to thy cross I cling."

Unfair!
Matthew 10:1-16

With me would you furrow your brow, wrinkle your nose, scrunch together your eyebrows, clench your fist, snarl and say, "Unfair!" Unfair! Some things just aren't fair!

When I was in the fourth grade, I had it made. I was the "teacher's pet." I was the teacher's pet because I did everything necessary to be her favorite. I enjoyed all the privileges indicative of my status of merited favoritism. I dusted the erasers and I took messages to the office, until Dennis Houk moved to Walnut Park Grammar School. Then he quickly became "teacher's pet" and assumed my former status.

It wasn't because Dennis was good. He was as mean as a striped snake. He was always pulling Kay Lester's hair, knocking books out of others' hands, and introduced us to a few "words" he had learned from his older brothers. I don't know why he became Mrs. Wright's favorite. Maybe she liked him better than she did me, or he was more fun-loving, or maybe it was easier to give him something to do to try to keep him out of trouble. But he became teacher's pet. Some things just aren't fair.

When I was fifteen, I had it made. My life was centered on three things: band, baseball, and Janice. I was a member, third chair trombone, of the Emma Sansom High School Rebel Marching Band - V.F.W. National Champions three years running. I also was the third baseman on the Alabama City Bank Pony League Baseball Team, defending League Champions with a 20-1 record. And there was Janice, a majorette in the band and my girlfriend.

Life was good until one day Dad came in and said, "All right, crew, pack it up. We are moving to Boaz, Alabama." I said, "Boaz, Alabama? You've got to be kidding, Dad!" He said, "Well, really it is not - Boaz, Alabama. It is Route 5, Boaz, Alabama. It's Sardis, Alabama!" I said, "Daddy, not Sardis! They don't even has a baseball team and their band can't blow their nose. Surely not, Dad! Surely not!" Unfair!

But we moved away. Someone else sat third chair, someone else played third base, and someone else married Janice. Don't you sometimes get tired of the people up there who make decisions that are dropped down on us, and we have to do what they say whether we want to or not? Some things just aren't fair!

From 1973 to 1983, I dreamed about the First Baptist Church of Gardendale. That was the church God was going to give to me! When an opportunity arose, I would drive by and lust after that pastorate. During a youth service in my church, the guest speaker - unaware of my envious dream - turned to me and said, "Did you know that the pastor of Gardendale resigned this morning? You know, you would make an excellent pastor for that church. My parents are influential there. I am going to recommend your"

"Thank you, Lord! My dreams are your dreams."

Three months later, I gazed into the congregation and, sure enough, there sat the Pastor Selection Committee of the First Baptist Church of Gardendale. I preached a stem-winder of a sermon. I was never better! The music was great, the service was spiritually moving, and additions were added. "Thank you, Lord! It's in the making!"

And they never came back!! Gave it to some other guy. I think he politicked for it a lot or something! Some things just aren't fair!

What if you and I were Hebrews in the first century? For twelve centuries, give or take a day or two, we have been God's chosen people -teacher's pet!" We have received the word of God, observed it, recorded it, kept it, interpreted it, and suffered because of it. Now all of a sudden we are no longer seen as God's only special people - teacher's pet with all its merited and favored status. They want to let other folks in who haven't paid the price we have paid! And they have the same rights and privileges!?

These are people who look funny, dress funny, eat funny, and smell bad. They are different from us! They know nothing about our sanitary rules, our liturgical procedures, our sacrificial system, our Law! They don't know an introit from a benediction and now we have got to let those people in? It isn't fair? And if we let them in, where is it going to stop? If we open the door to them, one day we will to let in those who wave their hands in worship, practice faith healing, and some may even believe in women preachers! Now I ask you, "Is that fair?"

The disgruntled laborers do have a point, do they not? For twelve long, hot, tiring hours they have labored in the vineyard and they received the same amount as those who have only worked one single hour. Not only that! Not only have they done twelve times as much work, they were paid last! They had to stand and watch the people who only worked an hour receive equal pay and get it before they do! Is that fair?

They have a point. I believe they were treated unfairly, don't you? But the real question is, by whom were they treated unfairly? The owner? No! He honored his word. He kept his contract. He gave everyone exactly what he said he would. No one was cheated. If anything, he would have to be considered generous. Then who treated them unfairly?

Would you entertain this thought? They treated themselves unfairly. The disgruntled laborers were unfair to themselves. Are we not sometimes guilty of the same thing when we engage in silly comparisons?

Is it not true that there always will be people who have more than we have, and there always will be people who have less than we have? Is it not also true that when I compare myself to people who have less than I have, I come away with the feeling of smugness and false superiority? Is it not also true that when I compare myself to people who have more than I have, I come away with the feeling of jealousy and envy?

Who said that my experience has to become the standard by which others are compared? If I compare myself to you, am I not at least in some way robbing you, or seeking to rob you, of your own uniqueness in God's sight and refusing to let you be the person God has created you to be? Are we not unfair to ourselves when we compare ourselves to others? Are we not unfair to ourselves and unfair to others when we fail to celebrate the goodness of God in their lives? When God has blessed them, are we not unfair to them when we fail to affirm and celebrate that?

We still have trouble with grace, especially when it is extended to others. It is all right when the care package is delivered to my front door, but what happens when the care package is delivered to my neighbor's front door? Are we sometimes envious when God is generous to others? Are we not refusing to let God be God?

I hated Ed Wheeler. Ed Wheeler was a member of Dr. Lunceford's philosophy class at Samford University when I was a struggling student. Every day in class Ed would fall fast asleep. Out like a light! Slept the entire hour every single day - made straight A's! He is a professor somewhere now. I worked myself to the bone in that class and just barely got by. How easy it would be to be envious of Ed Wheeler. How easy it would be to be envious when someone else becomes teacher's pet, sits third chair, plays third base, marries our girlfriend, or receives the church we thought we had to have. Unfair?

Jennifer Jones won an Academy Award for the title role in the movie, *The Song of Bernadette*. Bernadette has received a vision of the Immaculate Conception and has become quite a celebrity. An older nun is consumed by envy toward young Bernadette. In vaguely subdued anger the nun prays to God, "Why her? No one has prayed harder, worked longer, suffered greater than I. Why *her* and not *me*."

Later in the film Bernadette collapses while scrubbing the floor. After his examination, the doctor talks to the older nun. "Has she never complained?" "No, she just quietly does her work." The doctor continued, "That's amazing. The affliction she has, she has had a very long time. The pain is unbearable." Later the older nun prays to her Lord, "God, forgive me. Thank you for the opportunity of serving the one you have chosen."

Why can't we cease to engage in silly comparisons and rejoice that we are chosen at all7 Why can't we affirm the goodness of God toward some- one else and rejoice in the goodness of God in our own lives? What difference does it make if we are paid for one hour of work, or twelve hours of work; whether we are first or last? Why can't we just rejoice in God's goodness that we, too, are included as workers in His vineyard? "Why can't we quit engaging in silly comparisons and rejoice in the goodness that God extends to others and try to extend some of that goodness ourselves?

Dennis Houk became my best friend. I lost Janice, but I found Sharlon; and she has been the best thing that ever happened to me. And as bad as I hate to admit it, David Dykes did a wonderful job at First Baptist Church, Gardendale! Much better than I ever could have done. Then I was fortunate enough in God's grace to be called to First Baptist Church of Chattanooga. So I have received more than my just desserts. I have not received justice. I have received mercy. I have not received a just judgment; I have received grace. Thank God.

Grumbling about Grace
Matthew 20: 1-16

I had just graduated from Samford University and was working at Trophy Dairy to earn money to go to Seminary. Trophy Dairy was where they packaged milk.

One day the foreman came to me and said, "Come with me," We got into a pickup truck that had Trophy Dairy written on the side of it and went to the Old Depot in Gadsden, When we arrived at the Old Depot we saw about ten to twelve men sorta lollygagging around. The foreman in the pickup truck with Trophy Dairy written on the side of it stopped and cried out holding up four fingers. As he did so, here they came. Some came running, some came out-running the others until you jumped into the back of the pickup truck and we carried them off because they were to work at the dairy that day. Some out-ran others, some started to run and saw that they were being out-run and ran no further; I could not help but look and think about those faces and wonder since they did not work that day would they and their families eat that day.

It is in a very similar context that Jesus tells the parable of the workers in the vineyard. Now Jesus has already told his disciples that this Kingdom of God business that he has come to set about in the world is going to be radically different than the life that they were now living. The Kingdom of God wants to be this radical concept; this totally completely different concept. I mean the rich young ruler came to Jesus and he had never done anything wrong and he had lots of money and Jesus says, "You are not going to make it." And they said in the 19th chapter of Matthew. "If he can't be saved, then who in the world can be saved?" Jesus said, "You have got to remember that the first shall be last and the last, and the last shall be first."

They were so totally perplexed by this Kingdom of God that was so radically different than anything they could imagine. Then Jesus tells this parable, a parable where some workers were hired at six o'clock in the morning and worked all day long for a fair days wage and that day that meant that their family would eat that day. But then he went out at nine o'clock in the morning, twelve o'clock in the morning, three o'clock in the afternoon and five o' clock in the afternoon and hired other groups of people. But, yet, when it came time to pay them, he paid each and everyone the same; a fair days wage even though some only worked one hour. That meant that their families would eat as well. When we first see and hear that parable, we think that is just not right. That is unfair! How could you treat people like this?

Barbara Brown Taylor has a wonderful sermon on this passage of scripture and she said that this parable is like cod liver oil. We know that Jesus is right and we know that it is probably good for us, but yet it still does not make it very easy to swallow.

This is a difficult passage. What does it mean? First of all let's talk about what it does not mean. It is not applying to corporate economics or the way that Christians should treat their employees. You can't run a business like this. If you paid people who only worked one month the very same salary that you paid people who worked twelve months; you would be out of business in a hurry. Or if you had a class and you gave an "A" to the student who enrolled on the final day of the class the same grade as you gave those students who studied and worked hard all semester long; you would have a revolt. This is not the way Christians treat their employees. It is not about corporate economics.

This parable has a shock value. It is to shock us into thinking differently about life, about ourselves, about other people, and to think about this thing that Jesus called the Kingdom of God. A place that is radically different from life as we know it - the Kingdom of God. The whole concept of Jesus' teaching, the overriding metaphor, the simile that gives structure and discipline to all of Jesus' teachings is the Kingdom of God. What is this Kingdom of God like? Well, it is radically different in the way you now live.

So, Jesus tells a very radically impractical parable to cause us to think in different ways. First of all about God, himself. Because Jesus wants us to think in some ways that God is like the landowner. He is not the landowner, but in some ways he is like the landowner. Certain aspects of God's character is like the character of the landowner. For example, the landowner is always concerned about the laborers. He is not so much concerned about the harvest. He is not so much concerned about his crops. He is not so much concerned about his profit as he is concerned about the laborer.

He meets with the first group. They reach a negotiation. They are to work all day long for a denarius, a fair days wage in that day. But yet there are others who come and work half a day or part of a day or only one hour and he gives each one the same. The second group who come at nine o'clock, twelve o'clock, three o'clock and five o'clock come and the landowner says I will pay you what is right. The last, the ones who only work an hour, are just happy to get to work any at all. You see his concern is that everybody has a job and everybody is able to work. That meant that everyone would be able to feed their family that evening. That is what he is concerned about.

It is as if the landowner, God, the divine employer, is concerned about the poor, the outcast, those who are neglected and forgotten. Those who could only work an hour are paid equally to those who could work twelve hours.

Several years ago I used to help coach my sons in Little League. They had a rule in that league in Huntsville that every player, no matter how good or how bad, had to play two innings of a six-inning ball game. Everyone had to play two innings no matter how good or how bad you were. We had a pretty good team. In fact, we were playing for the league championship when all of a sudden we looked over there in the other dugout and the manager was making his players change jerseys. This allowed him to have his good players in the game all of the time and his players who were not quite so .good would not even get to play. He was cheating! Well, they caught him and banned him from that ballpark forever and rightfully so. But I thought, "Think what that said to those boys who could not play. You are not good enough. You don't belong. You are not as good as the others, so you are just the outcast, the throwaways. You don't matter."

The landowner in the parable is saying that everybody matters. Everybody should have an opportunity to work and everybody should have an opportunity to be able to feed their families. So, he is saying that God is like that and it causes us to think in different ways about the character and personality of God. It also enables us to think a little bit differently about how we relate to this kind of God. You see, the first group came and they were the negotiators. They had their contracts. They had their rule books. They had their job descriptions and they said we are going to work twelve hours and this is how much money we want and that is it that is wonderful!

The second, third, fourth group came and the landowner said that whatever was right I will pay you. And they just had to trust him to .do so. They were really guaranteed nothing. And the one-hour group was just happy to work at all. They did not know how much they were going to get. They just trusted the landowner to be able to work for an hour and be paid whatever. Something was better than nothing.

You see here is a contrast between two groups. The first group comes up and they say this is what we want. We are negotiating a deal. We want what we deserve. We want what is rightfully ours and we are going to work for that and that is exactly what we expect out of you. And God says that is exactly what you are going to get. These are the ones who said I want what is mine and I want what I deserve and when the others come and they get the same thing they say, "Hey, what is this? Wait just a minute. We worked longer than they did and you are giving them the same thing. What is going on here?" The landowner said, "Did I not give you what I promised you? Are you angry because I am generous? Don't I have the right to do with what I have, as I will? I mean is my generosity showing up the poverty of your own spirit? Are you mad because I am generous?" And the answer is, "Yes!"

They are angry. It is sorta like the Jews to a certain extent. The Jews are the ones who held the traditions, preserved the Old Testament, as we know it, and suffered because they were the people of God. But then all of a sudden they started letting the Christians in and they say, "Hey, what is going on here?" It is sorta like the apostles. They were the ones who left home and followed Jesus for years and years and years. Then all of a sudden they start letting in these new people and the apostles say, "Hey, wait a minute! What is going on here?"

It is like Jewish Christians in the book of Acts in the early part of the church. They were the ones who had followed Jesus for years and years and years arid they were the ones who had observed the Jewish law, they were the ones who had gone through the initiatory rights and all of a sudden they started letting the Gentile Christians be a part. They say, "Hey, wait a minute! What is going on here?" It is sorta like some people in the church. They say, "Hey, wait a minute! What is going on here? You mean you are going to let them in? Those people who are not like we are, who do not dress like we dress, or talk like we talk. I mean these are people who don't know a benediction from an introit. They think that John 3:16 is a restroom on the third floor of the education building. They don't know anything that we know. We are going to let them in the way they dress, the way they sing, the way they act, the way they worship? You are going to let them in? Wait a minute! What is going on here?

Several years ago I was in a different church and that church was growing. Sunday School needed some space and we were thinking about doing what this church did forty years ago. We were planning to divide the Fellowship Hall off with partition and make Sunday School classrooms. You divide it off with partitions! Some woman came to me and said, "No, you are not! You are not going to do that. I have been here all these years and I paid for that Fellowship Hall and it is going to stay a Fellowship Hall and it is not going to be a Sunday School classroom." I said, "Okay!" It stayed a Fellowship Hall.

Wait a minute! What are these people doing here? It is sorta like you are reared in a home and then all of a sudden when you are sixteen years of age your parents say, "Welcome to the family. We have just adopted your brother, who is also sixteen years of age." A year later they draw up their wills and everybody gets an equal share. Are you happy? You say, "Wait a minute! He didn't mow the yard. Wait a minute! He didn't take paregoric as a kid as I did. He didn't baby-sit the younger sister. Wait a minute!" Are you happy? NO! You are not happy.

You see this parable teaches us a way to think about God in just a little bit of different way. But also to think about how we relate to this God of amazing grace and mercy and also to think a little bit differently about the way we think about others. He gave to each a daily wage. That is what he gave - a daily wage. Well, for them it was a denarius. It enabled them to live another day. For the Christian it was much, much more than that.

Already in the ninth chapter he has said the first one of you has not given up a single thing for the Kingdom of God that will not be rewarded a hundred fold. And then he talks about what that daily wage is for the Christian. It is never ending, eternal, everlasting life. That is our wage as a Christian. We are literally drenched in God's grace each and every day of our lives. Everything that we have is literally drenched in the very grace of God. Even the precious life that we live is a gift of God. Can you think what a marvelous wonderful thing that we have - just the gift of life? That we can live each and every day on this wonderful place that God has created for us. And every time that we get pessimistic or negative we need to think about what a marvelous gift that God has given to each and every one of us – the gift of life itself.

John Claypool has a minister friend who had a family in his church with four children. The fifth child was born tragically and in such a way that the little girl had no arms and no legs, she lived until she was 21 years of age. She was a child that was a delight to be around. She had a wonderful sense of humor and a very alert mind. She had a lot of friends. People came just to be around her. She was such a delightful individual. She could not feed, dress herself or do any of the things that we take for granted. One time her older brother brought a friend home for Easter and he asked her, "Why do you not cry out with anger against what has been done to you?" She said, "I am able to see, taste, touch, and feel. I have been exposed to the finest literature in the world. I hear some of the most beautiful music in the world. I have friends. When I think of not being born; of not having life at all- even though some people may not think I have much - I have a lot! And I would not have missed the opportunity to be born for anything; life is God's gift to us. It is sorta like the Kris Kristopherson song, "Why me Lord, What have I ever done to deserve even one of the kindness you've shown?" And the answer is of course, Well - you know what the answer is.

The parable tells us that we are inheritors, heirs of God, joint heirs with Jesus Christ. Everything Jesus has in heaven one day shall be yours and today we enjoy the blessed gift of life. We enjoy God's love and grace, his mercy, his forgiveness, the opportunity to walk and live amongst his people. How drenched, literally, we are in the marvelous amazing grace of God each and every day. It is God's grace to give out, as he will. It is his. The earth is the Lord's and the fullness thereof and all gifts therein belong to him and he gives them, as he wills. It is a very, very difficult concept for some of us to grasp, but the bottom line is that God is generous. He is generous to those of us who don't deserve it and if anyone does deserve it he is generous to them also. Luke said that God is gracious to the unkind and the unforgiving. God is generous! The question is. How do we feel about that? We are sometimes very happy when God's generosity is bestowed upon us, but what about when God's generosity is bestowed upon those that we do riot think are deserving. Sometimes we even compare ourselves to other people. And God says; "I love everybody." And God is generous and gives to each and every one of us, as he wills.

It is like the fable told of the little boy whose mother is was very ill. He gathered together what few pennies he had and went to the village to buy her some flowers. She loved flowers. When he got to the village he found that there were none for sale. He was distraught and distressed. He wanted to do that for his mother, but he was unable to do so. On the way home he passed by this beautiful garden. He could not believe how beautiful that garden was. There were roses everywhere in full bloom. He stopped the manager and asked, "Can I buy some of these flowers?" The manager said, "No, you cannot. These flowers belong to the King. They are not for sale," With that the little boy walked off crying. His last hope was gone when a voice was heard behind him. It was the Prince, the son of the King, and he said, "You are exactly right. These flowers are not for sale. They belong to the King. But he does give them away." With that the little boy turned around and the Prince loaded up both arms with long beautiful red roses to be given as a gift - a grace gift - for his mother.

The Longest Journey
Matthew 21:28-32

Jesus asked the question, "What do you think? " It is important what you think. "Mrs. Jones, this is the fifth vote and we're not going to take another. Eleven of us say this man is guilty. You say he is innocent. We're going to vote one more time and if you do not change your vote then we have a hung jury. This murderer is going to be retried and very possibly could go free." What do you think?

"Mrs. Smith, we know that you are our newest deacon. We feel a little reluctant to ask you to make this decision, but our deacon board is divided; three and three. You're going to cast the deciding vote of whether or not we let this first black family into our fellowship." You have the vote. What do you think?

"Mother, you have such good advice in these matters. I really don't know what God is calling me to do. I feel that God wants me to go to medical school and I feel that God wants me to go seminary. Every time I pray I receive no direction from the Lord as to which road to take. Tell me mother, "What do you think?"

It matters what you say. It matters for you. It matters for others. It matters what you think and it also matters what you do. The longest journey we take is from head to our heart. There are many things we know we should do. Many times it takes a long time for a message to get from our head to our heart and then to our feet. The longest journey you will ever take is to take the message "I know. I know." And let it be translated into concrete action.

What do you think? That was the question that Jesus posed to the scribes and Pharisees with which he was embroiled in a controversy. They were questioning Him in Verse 23 of the same chapter. "By what authority are you doing all of this?" Jesus said, "Well, I'll answer that if you will answer this: By what authority did John the Baptist perform his works? Was it of heaven or of men?" They were trapped. If they said of heaven then Jesus would ask, "Well, why did you not respond?" If they said of men then that would put them in trouble with the people. So, they said, "Got me." Then Jesus said, "Then I will not tell you by what authority I do these things."

Jesus continued, let me tell you a story. What do you think? Then Jesus told them a parable about practice and profession; about finishers and starters; about one person who said yes with his mouth but no with his life, and another person who said no with his mouth, but yes with his life. Then he asked which did what was right. Again, they were trapped. Well, the one who did the will of the Father was the one who initially said no, but went ahead and did what was right. That's much better than the one who said yes but didn't do anything."

What do you think? You might say that 'both were wrong and you're right. Both were wrong. How and why would a person say yes with their mouth and no with their life? Why would a person initially say, "Yes, of course, I'll be happy to do that?" But then their commitment fizzles and they do nothing.

Possibly he wanted to get his father off his case. "Well, if I tell the old man I'll go ahead and do it, he'll get off my back" never once intending to do what his father asked him to do; knowing all along that eventually he would be caught. How in the world can someone do that? George Elliott in her book, *Silas Marner* talks about the "religion of chance." She talks about people who deliberately and willfully do things they know they shouldn't do. Then they pray to the "God of chance" that somehow the world will come to an end or Jesus will come back or something will happen and they will not have to suffer the consequences of their misdeeds. "The religion of chance."

Perhaps, he meant to obey. He had good intentions. There's a road paved with that. He had good intentions, but he began to find excuse. I really don't feel well. My neighbor is sick and Aunt Nancy's half-cousin's brother's sister is in the hospital and I need to be with them." He had good intentions. Things just crept in and those good intentions got lost somewhere. It is these little habits that are often the beginning of life patterns of behavior.

Perhaps, he was caught in a moment when he had to say something and he panicked, similar to a foxhole resolve or a sick bed promise. "The old man caught me off guard and I had to say something." And, then after the crisis is over the resolve is forgotten, the promise goes away. Aren't we sometimes like that? Do we sometimes say yes with our mouth, but no with our life? Our profession is much better than our practice?

Often churches find themselves in that kind of predicament when they say, "Yes, Lord, we will minister to our community. We will devote our time and energy to reaching, our community for Christ." But what happens when the demands come, money has to be paid, the bills have to be met, the time has to be given, and the investment of resources has to be allotted. "Well, Lord, it is just easier to go and do it where it is easier." Many times churches spend all of their time and their resources building beautiful buildings in nice comfortable suburbs. Someone has called the suburb the "ghetto of forgetfulness." I can identify with that as a church person, and I can identify with that as a person. When I think of all the diets I've started and never completed. When I think of all the letters I've left half written and of all the books I've left half read, I can identify with that. Can you? What do you think?

The other son was wrong as well. He said no with his mouth, but yet he said yes with his life. He was poor in his profession, but he was pretty doggone good in his practice. Now how could one do that? First of all, the son had to say, "I was wrong." He had to swallow his pride and say, "I should not have told my father that." The Pharisees to whom this was directed could not say they were wrong. They had all the answers. Hundreds of years of tradition and they have all the answers. Their ritual said they had all the answers. The law said they had all the answers. Their regulations said they had all the answers, and they could not say, "I was wrong." That is not just an affliction of the aged or of the religious.

I went to college with many people who at twenty-one years of age had all the answers. Twenty-one years of age they had all the answers-seven steps to anything you want to know. Three points to anything you want to ask and an answer for every question. It was as if at age twenty-one they found out everything and the rest of their lives would be spent mentally and spiritually dead from the neck up.

"I was wrong." By his actions he said, "I'm sorry." Whether he went to the father or not and said, "I'm sorry," I don't know. He said it with his life. "I was wrong." How hard and difficult the mouth finds it to fashion those words: I'm sorry, I was wrong. The whole world stands on the precipice of war because one ruler in the East cannot say I was wrong. I'm sorry. The heart of the matter is I don't know why the first son said yes and then no and I'm not quite sure I know why one could say no and then yes. I think it might be that the first son, the one who said no and then said yes, was able to re-examine a decision that he had already made as to its validity. He was to go back over past behavior and with objectivity look at that and say, "I blew it. I need to change my mind."

In a book about Lyndon Johnson called *Lyndon: An Oral Biography*, he is quoted when questioned about the Viet-Nam conflict. "I never really felt I had the luxury of re-examining my decisions. Once the commitment was made to use force, we spent all of our time and energies in trying to validate that decision and somehow prove that it was a good one." I never had the luxury of re-examining my decision. How sad. What would God say about that? He says you always have the luxury of re-examining your decision. Don't let the past tie you down particularly if that past is wrong. Don't let a decision in the past, if it's a bad one, continue to make your present and future even worse. God understands. God knows we're going to fail. God knows we're going to blow it. God knows we're going to make mistakes, that's why He sent His son, Jesus. He knows we're sinners. He knows we're going to make bad decisions. God is fully aware of the fact that we grow through trial and error. Part of growth is error and part of error is admitting that error and then rectifying it. God understands that. He gives us the luxury to re-examine old decisions and make them right. An individual once asked Mahatma Gandhi "Why are you saying this? You are so inconsistent. Last week I heard you say something and it was completely the opposite of what you're saying today. How can you be so inconsistent?" Gandhi replied, "My friend, in the last week I learned something." What do you think? Can we learn something? Is that not the process of spiritual growth: of learning through trial and error, admitting our error, capitalizing on our good decisions and going on? If not, what is the opposite?

A friend of mine told me this and it's so classic I have to tell you. I could not believe anyone would actually say it this way. A pastor was making a concentrated effort to bathe his worship service in Scripture. Scripture was read two and three times in the service. One of his members came to him and said, "Preacher, we have got to stop reading those Scriptures in worship that disagree with what we believe." Think about it.

That's opposite. "I have all the answers. I know it all, and I'm certainly not going to let Scripture interfere with my belief." The alternative is to be open to God. God is alive and vibrant in the present. The alternative is to be open to His Word which is alive and vibrant in the present and let God grow us through the process of trial and error. What He's really saying is you do not have to be bound by decisions in the past that were wrong. Isn't that good news? Isn't that wonderful news? No matter how many times you have said no to God in the past you can say yes to God today.

Both sons we're wrong. We know that. Maybe there is another way, a better way. Fred Craddock tells the story of Jimmy who is about so high. Had just gotten his first baseball glove. "Got me a new glove." Jimmy is all excited. He's so excited because he is about to go in just a few short days to his first Little League baseball practice. "Dad, are you sure it is Thursday at 5: 30?" "Yes, Jimmy, I'm positive." "Better call the coach just to make sure." "Coach, this is Jimmy. Is it Thursday?" "Yes, Jimmy Thursday." "I'll be there Coach."

The next day on Tuesday he goes to his mother. "Mother, are you sure Thursday and not Tuesday?" "This Thursday at 5:30." "Better call the coach just to make sure." "Yes, Jimmy, call the coach just to make sure." "Jimmy, Thursday at 5:30." "I'll be there, coach." On Wednesday he begins to think they might have changed the time of practice. Better call the coach. "Jimmy, it is tomorrow, Thursday at 5:30." "I'll be there, Coach." Thursday finally arrives. About 4:00 clouds begin to gather in the sky and about 5:00 it begins to sprinkle a little. At 5:15 it's pouring and at 5:30 it's coming down in sheets, flash flood warnings are flashing.

The coach's wife is setting the table. They live right across from the practice field. She looks out the window and says, "Honey, come here. Isn't that Jimmy out there in the rain where home plate used to be?" "My gracious, I believe it is." He puts on his rain coat and hat, grabs an umbrella, and swims across the field. There is Jimmy standing in front of the backstop where home plate used to be. "Jimmy, what in the world are you doing here?" To which he said, "Coach, I told you I'd be here."

Now I know and you know, after he sits under our teaching and preaching and parenting, one day Jimmy will learn to say, "Well, I'll be there if it doesn't rain, or if I don't have somewhere to go or if I feel okay. If everything just fits in, I might drop by sometime Thursday." He'll learn. Most of us have. But I truly think that within that little boy's commitment to integrity could be the secret to change a life. It could be the commitment that changed a family. It could be the commitment that changes the world.

R.S.V.P.
Matthew 22:1-14

Once upon a time I was sitting in a worship service in the back of the church. It was a little country church with no air conditioning, windows were up, and a nice little breeze was blowing in and through the small congregation. The pastor was preaching on his favorite text. The text read: "When in doubt go the old, true, and tried way. A bird in the hand is worth two in the bush. Better be safe than sorry." He preached on that text quite often. He was very comfortable with it. The congregation was very comfortable with it. I was very comfortable with it. In fact, I was so comfortable with it I was about to go to sleep.

Just as I was about to doze off, I heard a voice from outside the window. It was saying, "Gary, Gary." As I looked out the window, I saw an individual saying. "Come with me. Come follow me." "What?" "Come with me, and I will show you a place where shepherds risk their own lives and the safety of ninety-nine sheep to look for the one that he loves that is lost. I will show you a place where an individual finds a pearl of great price and sells everything he has to purchase that one pearl. I will show you a place where a man finds a treasure, hides it in a field and sells everything he has to buy that field." I said, "There is no such place." "Oh yes, there is." He said. "Come with me. Follow me and I will take you to a place where there is a party. It's going on all the time and everyone is invited. Everyone and anyone is invited; tax collectors, thieves, prostitutes, and prodigals coming home from wasted journeys. Everyone is invited and you're invited. Come along with me. "Ah, there is no such place." With that he left.

As I put my head on the side of the pew to try to go back to sleep. I had a strange feeling in my heart that kept me from returning to sleep. Such haunting words he said. At the end of the service, I shook hands with the preacher at the back door. He shook my hand and said, "What was all that commotion going on back there during the service?" I said, "There was a man outside the window with dark hair, dark piercing eyes, and a dark beard. He had on a funny looking robe. He had twelve guys with him, and he wanted me to go with him." "You're kidding." "No, I'm not kidding. He wanted me to go with him. He said, "If I would follow him, he would take me to a place where shepherds risk all they have, people sell all they have just to get a field, just to get a pearl, and where there's a party going on all the time. Everyone is invited; good, bad, rich and poor. EVERYONE IS INVITED."

Then the preacher said something that to be honest with you caught me off guard. He said. "I've heard of such a place and I've longed for such a place. Do you think we can go with him?" I don't know," I said, "he's already gone but we might could find him." "Would you like to go?" 'With that the preacher and I set off to find the man and his twelve companions who invited us to a land that stirred our imagination.

We got lost. We found an individual and inquired, "Have you seen a man walking by here with dark hair, piercing eyes, dark beard, robe, has twelve guys with him and says he's on his way to a party. Have you seen him?" "Oh, that party. Yes, I've seen him. I know that party. It is the kingdom party. Are you going?" "We would like to go. How do you get there?" He said, "You see those footsteps?" "Yes!" "You just follow those footsteps. They'll take you to the party." "How will we know when we get there?" "You'll know. You'll know."

Sure enough my preacher friend and I followed the steps and when we got there was no disguising what was happening. There was a party going on and I mean a party like you have never seen in all of life. People were arrayed in beautiful garments. Everyone was having a great time.

There was laughter, joy, love, peace and hospitality. It was a party like I've never seen in all of my life. My preacher said, "I wonder how you get into this party?" I said, "I don't know, but let's watch others as they come." The closer we got to the party, we saw the guy with the black hair, black beard, robe and the piercing eyes. He was the host. We noticed a woman who came up to the porch as we stood off to the side and watched.

This lady was painted up, make-up half inch thick, big, huge earrings and her hair was really fixed up. She was dressed fit to kill and she had under her arm a bottle. I said, "Well, she's bringing a bottle of wine to the host." I looked again and saw that it wasn't a bottle of wine at all. It was a bottle of water. She said to the host, "Do you remember me? We talked at Jacob's well once. Do you remember me?" With that the host broke into a great smile and said, "Of course, I remember you. How are things in Samaria? You gave me water there too, didn't you?" She said, "Is there room for me in your party?" He said, "Of course, there's room for you. By the way, did you ever marry the sixth husband? Come on into the party."

Then a big Rolls Royce drove up. This guy got out, a short guy. He, too, was dressed fit to kill. His chauffer was standing at the Rolls Royce, with a money belt around his waist that would choke a horse. The man was SHORT, I mean very SHORT. He walked up to the host and said, "Do you have room in the party for a reformed tax collector?" With that the host broke into a smile again and said, "Of course, Zacchaeus, I have room. It will be a joy for me to be your host. You were once a host to me. Come on in to the party. Welcome! Welcome!"

The next person that came up, well, she looked just a little bit out of place if you know what I mean. Her hair was a mess, and lipstick was smeared all over her face. Her clothes, what little she had on, were just hanging on her. Her arms were red and bruised like where someone had grabbed her and dragged her. She came up to the host with her head down looking at the ground. She said, "I know I look a mess. They caught me in the very act and I know that you don't have room for me in your party." With that the host smiled and said, "Of course, I do. I've got room for you. Of course. I wish you would put on a housecoat, but come on in."

My preacher friend and I were about to see if we could get in when all of a sudden the crowd was separated as this nice handsome man walk- ed up to the porch. He walked up to the host, very handsome, wonderfully dressed, and he began to speak. You could tell that this was a man of education and articulation. I know I can come. You see I'm rich. I'm a ruler. I have kept the law since I was a small child. I know that I am welcome to the party," as he started. "Into the party," the host said, "Wait a minute! Wait just a moment. You see you cannot come into the party yet." "Why?" "For you to come into the party, you must sell all you have and give to the poor." "What?" You let the others in. You let in the painted lady and the short thief. The woman taken in an adulterous act, you even let her in. And you're not letting me in? They didn't have to do anything." "Oh yes, they did," the host said. "Oh yes, they did." "The painted lady started a revival with her testimony. She told everybody what I had done for her. The short tax collector gave back four-fold to anyone that he cheated. Even the woman caught in the intimate act was told to repent, change her ways and not to sin anymore. Oh, yes, there was something that was required of all of them. And there is something that is required of you."

You are welcome to come, but there is something that is required of you. You must sell all you have and give it to the poor." Jesus says, "Come! Come! Come; black and white, male and female, red and yellow, slave, free, poor, rich, educated, uneducated. COME!" Everyone come. Anyone and everyone, you are welcome to the banquet and anyone can come to the party. Come to the party! Come now! Come! But don't' come. Don't come unless ... Come all of you, painted ladies, short thieves, and adulterous people. Come rich young ruler. Come sleeping worshipper. Let the burned out preacher come. Let everyone come, but don't come unless you are willing to wear the wedding garment of God's righteousness. Do not come unless you are willing to be changed unless you are willing to let Him change you. Because if we put him first, if we repent of our sins, if we ask Him to come into our life, if we put Him first that means we put everything else second. EVERYTHING! Don't come unless you are willing to do that and remember it is such a painful thing. Change is such a painful thing.

A tiny flower whose petals could be crushed from the heat of a child's hand, in the spring pushes its way up through dirt, grit, grass, gravel, rock and spurts its head up out of the ground. Do you feel the pain in that? Change is a painful thing. We talk a lot about it glibly but change is painful and the choice we make to change is never that simple. Oh, we preachers go on and on, "Choose between Jesus and the Devil. Jesus and the Devil! Jesus and the Devil!" But it's not that simple and you know it. I know it. Jesus knows it. The Bible knows it. Jesus knows that change is painful. Often the choices we make are painful because we don't choose between Jesus and the Devil. It's more, like between God and our preference. God and our habit. God and our job, God and our parents, God and our mate, God and our children. Difficult choices and painful choices. Jesus says, "Come you're welcome to come, but don't come, unless you're willing to change."

Come, but don't come unless you are willing to grow. Don't come unless you are willing to expose yourself to things that are different than the things you have been exposed to in order to grow. The parable of the wedding garment is really a parable within a parable. The parable of the banquet says COME. But the parable of the wedding garment is inserted by our Lord at the end of that parable and says, "Don't come unless you are willing to wear "the wedding garment." Everyone is welcome into the church, but not every kind of lifestyle is admissible in the church. There are some responsibilities to being a Christian. There is a path on which the Christian must walk. The Christian can't go in every direction. The Christian follows the footsteps to the party. Any other way, we lose our way. So he says, "Follow me." Be willing to change and grow.

E. Stanley Jones once preached a sermon entitled. "What God Has Taught Me So Far." I like that. We over play this childlikeness thing. There is a certain amount of childlikeness that we almost have if we come to Jesus. But we do not remain children. The Bible says child-likeness is appropriate, but grow up. GROW UP. Be willing to change. Be willing to grow if you want to be a part of my kingdom.

A little girl was awakened by her mother in the early hours of the morning. She had fallen asleep on the floor - never made it to bed. The mother gathered her up in her arms. "Honey, what are you doing here?" She said, "I guess I just fell asleep too close to the place I got in."

Don't come unless you are willing to grow. Don't come unless you are willing to change. Don't come unless you are willing to keep on - to persevere --to persist. Until what? Until He comes again or we meet Him through death, until, we carryon. We persist. We persevere!

There's a lot of talk today about the second coming. Prophets galore, prophecies abound, and all this stuff in the East. Well, it could be the end of time and the Lord may be coming again soon! But that's not the question. The question is not when He is coming. The question is what are we doing "in the meantime." There is a real risk that we as Christians take when we over concentrate upon the Second Coming of Christ. The risk is that we become so preoccupied with the Second Coming that we forget about His first coming and the responsibilities and the response that, it puts upon us right now, in some unknown and possibly even distant future. Don't come! Come everybody and anybody. But don't come unless you are willing to change or let God change you. Don't come unless you are willing to grow. Don't come unless you are willing to hang in there and persevere.

Forest Carter tells a story set in the rural South during the depression. A father is walking along the side of his house, well it is more like a shack. He hears his two daughters on the back porch and they're laughing loudly, shrieking with joy and glee. He decides to investigate. On the old back porch on the old wooden steps are his two daughters. They are looking through a Sear's Roebuck Catalog. In that catalog they see all of the beautiful clothes, all the bright colors, all the beautiful garments. They're laughing. The father comes up to the children and grabs the book from them. "Don't ever let me see you with this book again." He strikes them just a little on the leg and they ran into the house. The father then sits down on the back porch, buries his head in his hands and cries like a baby, He knows or thinks he knows that his daughters will never have the beautiful clothes in the beautiful book.

The first time I heard that I felt sorry for the father, but I think I have changed my mind. I do not think it is cruel for the daughters to see the beautiful clothes, the brightly colored dresses, the wonderful garments that they may or may not have, if and when they grow up. The garment they could wear may have a label that reads, "Made in Heaven."

Be Prepared
Matthew 25:1-13

We come today to recognize the hard work of so many, many people who have given of themselves in numerous ways to make this day possible. But we also come in realization that we now have before us opportunities that have never been ours. We are realizing afresh and anew what it is to be a center-city church in Chattanooga. This is not the end, but the beginning. This is not a conclusion, but a continuation. The vision continues. We come not today to pat ourselves on the back, but we come today to reaffirm and recommit ourselves to the calling of God to His people in this place and to reaffirm that mission and ministry as a center-city church. Recognition and realization.

I was privileged to attend a conference this past week in Dallas, Texas. Among those who attended the conference was Dr. Dan Yeary who was in our congregation a few years ago. Many of you perhaps know that this past year he moved to the pastorate of the North Phoenix Baptist Church. North Phoenix Baptist is one of the greatest and largest churches in the Southern Baptist Convention. We were so inquisitive and curious. We asked Dan to tell us about it. He said, "Well, we have fifteen hundred people on Sunday night, a thousand show up for Wednesday night services. For the past ten years they have baptized at least a thousand people a year. Then he said, "For the last five years we have been declining." When he said that our jaws fell open and our mouths exhibited the amazement we felt. And then he said, "I have the best 1950's church in the United States."

Now, I have no doubt that great man of God and those great people of God will build upon the foundation that has been placed by Dr. Richard Jackson and that church will prepare and position itself for the 1990's and the 21st Century. I feel in many ways that is what these past three years have been about.

As a church and as a people of faith, we are positioning ourselves and preparing ourselves for the 21st I Century. We are providing God with resources He never has had here before. And now we reaffirm and recommit ourselves to the rest of this decade and to the Third Millennium.

Preparedness - that is the topic about which our text speaks. Jesus said that they were having a wedding celebration, one of the most joyous and festive events in the life of any Hebrew family. Two groups of people attended. But the story did not begin there. The story began previous to that in decisions that those people made or did not make. One group of people, five maidens, made decisions like everything would be just the way it always had been. Nothing would be different, and everything would go according to schedule. Jesus called those five maidens "foolish." The other group of five maidens decided that they would make special preparation just in case things did not go as planned. Jesus called that group of five maidens "wise." And sure enough, exactly what the five wise maidens planned for, happened. The bridegroom, the one upon whom all of the celebration was dependent, delayed his coming and by delaying his coming he created a certain sense of crisis and uncertainty. When the bridegroom came he found five who were prepared for his coming. They went out and celebrated joyously with him. The five who were unprepared and could not celebrate missed the joy of the coming of the bridegroom.

Preparedness for an uncertain future. Prepare for uncertain times, be ready for a changing world because things may not be as they have always been. There is a way that we can prepare and be ready for whatever comes our way. For the past three years we have been preparing and positioning ourselves for mission and ministry. With the renovation of this Sanctuary, new lights and sound we have prepared ourselves for warm, energetic, celebrative music and worship.

With the obtaining of two brand new buses we have prepared ourselves to continue with existent ministries such as the Thursday shopping for the elderly, and to create new kinds of ministries similar to what the youth encountered last weekend as they went skiing in Gatlinburg. With a new playground and a new soccer and softball field we have prepared ourselves to minister and see that recreation and creation are all part of the same godly process. With a brand new recreation center, we have prepared to let the Word of God speak to all generations and to the total person. With the obtaining of a new elevator and chair lifts we have prepared for the people to negotiate almost the entirety of these buildings without ever having to maneuver a step. With added educational space and renovated educational space we have prepared for the future growth of our church and for times of fellowship and communion and Bible study around which people can grow spiritually. These are all ways in which we can reach out more effectively to our community. With new office space we are prepared for better staff communication enabling us to be more effective in ministering to our people. With a new music suite we are preparing ourselves for an expanding and ever growing music ministry which is so vital to everything we do here in this place. With new parking facilities we are prepared to welcome more and more people as they come to be a part of what God is doing here in this place.

With the renovation and so many countless hours of sweat equity at Dogwood Lodge, we are providing not only to our own people but to the entire community a place of Christian nurture and discipleship. Bookings are twice this year what they were last year. With a renovated library we are preparing ourselves to minister to all ages within our congregation to the written and spoken word. We have a new heating and air conditioning system, new carpeting. Renovation of the bride's room and so many, many other things that have been a part of this marvelous undertaking. We have the most beautiful gym floor I have ever seen. I hope within one year it is worn completely out by being in constant use.

We are building something here that is a testimony to the Glory of God, but we also have resources that are practical and useable and will help our people grow in so many ways. Preparation. We have prepared and now we are ready to accept the work that God has called us to do in whatever direction that may take and in whichever corner that may lead. We are here and we are ready to do as God has called us to do. We are ready to go where God has called us to go. That is challenging. It might mean standing beside Pilate, it might mean taking a dusty road down to Damascus. It could conceivably mean standing beside Mother Teresa in the streets of India or taking a trip to Korea. It might mean joining a jazzercise group or it might mean playing volleyball or softball. It could mean using facilities for Bible study and fellowship or serving in the downtown soup kitchen or putting up boards and nails on a Habitat for Humanity House. It might mean leading a backyard Bible club or Vacation Bible School during Mission Week, Chattanooga. It might mean going with a Friendship Class to the elderly in the buildings we call the Towers. It might mean being a part of a seminar at Dogwood Lodge. It could mean giving a word of encouragement, or a word of prayer, or a visit in a home saying, "I want to share with you the love and light of my life Jesus Christ my Lord."

Two people applied for a job. The interviewer asked one, "What can you do?" He responded simply, "I can do what I am told to do," He was hired. We are here today prepared to do what God has told us, called and equipped us to do, going forth in His power and in His love as the center-city church in Chattanooga to minister to this community in the name of Christ.

Before she was Mother Teresa she was Sister Teresa. When she was Sister Teresa she went to her superiors and said. "'Have a vision. I have three pennies and I have a vision to build an orphanage for my Lord." Her superiors said, "Three pennies. Are you kidding? What can you do with three pennies?" "Nothing?" Sister Teresa responded, "That is true, but with three pennies and God I can do anything."

We have our three pennies and we have God. Come on dreamers, we have work to do, Let us go with each other and let us go with God. The vision continues.

What to Do During the Delay
Matthew 25:1-13

What are YOU doing during the delay?

The University of Louisville Cardinal Basketball Team went to a tournament several years ago in Hawaii. At their first practice session in Maui they discovered that the managers had forgotten to bring basketballs. They looked around in dismay, and then heard a basketball bouncing outside the gym. They saw a young lad with an old battered, well-worn basketball. They tried to buy the basketball from the young man. "Ten dollars?" "No!" "Fifteen dollars? Twenty-five dollars? Fifty dollars?" "No! I'll not sell my basketball."

So the practice was delayed until they could purchase some basketballs. In the meantime one of the Cardinal players said to the little boy, "You know, fellow, you're dumb. You could have sold that basketball for fifty dollars." The little boy scratched his nose and said, "Well, mister, I may be dumb, but at least I'm smart enough to know that if you're going to practice basketball you need to bring a basketball."

Preparation, or the lack thereof, is part of the message that Jesus is speaking of in our text today. Preparation! Jesus told a story about a wedding. On the way to the wedding we find five young giggly teenagers, Now Sarah Nancy says to Bobbie Jo, (they're from Southern Israel), I just can't wait to get to the wedding, can you?" "No, it's the most exciting time of our year. A whole week-long of party, party!!" One says to the other, "In my wedding, I'm going to have ten bridesmaids just like this one. The other says, "You'll never get Billy Bob Steinberg to marry you, but when you do I want to be there." (Again, they're from Southern Israel).

"This is the right place that we're going to meet the others, is it not?" "Yes, right here at the Piggly Wiggly." They looked down the street and saw five other bridesmaid also going to the same wedding. But somehow they looked different. There's something about them that is unlike the five that are already there. They have something in their hand. Not only do they have a lantern in one hand, but they have a Clorox jar full of kerosene in the other. "What are you doing with that kerosene? You even smell like kerosene. You're going to a wedding like that?" "You never can tell," they said, "when you might run out of kerosene and we have plenty." "Oh, that will never happen!" "You never know." Sure enough the bridegroom was delayed.

Now isn't that just like life? Isn't that realistic? Things never happen when we think they're going to happen. And they never happen the way we think they're going to happen. Isn't that just like life?

A young couple is eagerly waiting for the transfer to come through. "If that transfer will just come, then we can sell our house and move to Atlanta. We know we're going to Atlanta, but we don't know when and we can't buy a house until we know. If we only knew, we could buy a house and get on with our life. But all we can do now is wait. WAIT! WAIT!

He is fifteen years, eleven months, one week, one day, seven hours and thirty-three seconds old and he cannot wait until that eventful day when he will be sixteen, then he can get a driver's license. But all he can do now is wait. WAIT! WAIT!

She is in her eighth month and her heart is filled with anticipation and anxiety during this last month. "Will that baby ever come?" All she can do now is wait. WAIT! WAIT!

Life is full of waiting. The children of Israel were forty years between Egypt and Canaan. In the meantime, they stumbled around in the desert and waited. Jesus was thirty years waiting on some signal from the father that now was the time. How any times did he look at the sunset and say, "Oh, Father, when?" All He could do was wait and wait. But is that all He did? Did, he just wait or did He actively wait? Did he wait with initiative? "Did he wait with intentionality? Did he wait aggressively?

All ten bridesmaids slept, but yet there was a difference in their slumber. One was a slumber that just dozed off. No preparation. Just sort of fell off to sleep, not thinking about what might happen ...no preparation, no extra oil!

But the other five went to sleep knowing full well that they had prepared. "No matter what comes we have our kerosene in our Clorox bottle. Whatever comes and however it might happen, we're ready. We're ready!"

Now who had the best sleep? One group was an actor...acting with intentionality, with initiative and with aggressiveness. The other group was reactors. No initiative. No aggressiveness. "Just let it happen ... when my big break comes ... when my ship comes in... when that phone call arrives then I'll have it made. Usually those who are unprepared depend upon chance-the luck of the draw, a surprise phone call, a break here and there. Yet there are others who live life with preparation, initiative and intentionality, knowing that most of the breaks we have we make ourselves. They usually happen when we are prepared.

If I were to ask you today, "Are you prepared?" What would you say? "Yeah, I'm prepared. I took out my earthquake insurance just a few days ago. I'm prepared" "Well yeah, I think I'm prepared to die. I think so. I feel confident in that." Others might say. "Well, you know I am prepared. I just finished my Christmas shopping." Another might say, "Yes, I'm prepared, we're going to have a turkey for Thanksgiving and the invitations are out!"

When you think of preparation, about what are you thinking? Are you thinking of being prepared for the worst; the earthquake on December 3 or 4. Death itself? Are you preparing for the best? What are we doing in the meantime? What are we doing during the delay? Most all of life is waiting and if Jesus continues to tarry we've got a while to wait.

What are we doing in the meantime? You know what God is doing in the meantime? He's pitching a party. God is pitching a party. God is throwing a party. You know that is what the church is all about. In the two thousand years that He has tarried. God created the church and He is now throwing party. It is a party for sinners. It's a party for the last, the least, the lost, and each of us. It is for you and it is for me. It is for silly little girls running .down the road with Clorox bottles full of kerosene. It is for every one of us. He is pitching a party. Are you coming? You are invited you know.

Karl Olsson in his wonderful little book, *Come to the Party*, talks about four groups of people. He says there is a group of people who do not even know about the party. Their life is so busy or whatever that they don't even know there's a party going on. Another group knows about the party, but they don't think they're invited. There is another group of people who know about the party and they might even go, but they do not deserve to stay. Then there is the fourth group. They know about the party. They go to the patty and stay and have a good time. Now in which group do you belong?

Robert Capon has an insightful comment when he says, "God is not your mother-in-law who comes snooping to see if your wedding present china is chipped. Rather He is more like a happy old uncle who appears at your door with a salami under one arm and a six pack of Coca Cola under the other, ready to party. Now which image of God do you have? God is having a good time. He is calling us to have a good time with Him. Are we preparing for the worst or are we preparing for the best?

Robert Louis Stevenson said, "To miss the joy is to miss all." Are you missing the joy? Did you come to the party and didn't feel that you belonged or deserved to stay? Have you just forgotten about the party? Or are you there having a good time? In those days the most festive occasion was a wedding. Some came prepared, some did not and then the door was shut. The bridegroom came at midnight. How many times do things happen when we least expect them?

Mark Twain said, "Often a long expected event takes the form of the unexpected when it comes." And he came unexpectedly as he will. He came unexpectedly and he found five who were ready for his coming. They filled their lamps again with the kerosene from the Clorox bottle, yet the others were unprepared. "Can we have some of your kerosene?" They responded, "No!" At first glance that seems unchristian. Yet this preparation is something that we have to do. No one can do it for us. It is personal. You have to do it. I have to do it. Mother cannot prepare for me. Father cannot prepare for you. WE DO IT OURSELVES. If we are prepared, we go to the party. If not, the door is shut. It's that simple.

My father told me that he was the second best football player he had even seen in over forty years of religiously watching high school football. I played three sports with him. I have never seen a finer athlete. In his senior year in high school, he not only starred in baseball, basketball and track, but for the second straight year he was an all-state running back in football. For the third straight year he was all-county. His senior year he rushed for well over a thousand yards and scored twenty-four touch downs. He was signed to a grant-in-aid by Auburn University. They were thrilled to sign him. Then they asked him to take an entrance exam. After that they had to say, "We are sorry, we're sorry."

Miss Jones you are the most qualified candidate we have had for this position. "As you can see this position has a wonderful salary, unlimited opportunities, advancements guaranteed, you have the personality, and the qualifications. We're excited about your coming to work for us. However, there is one minor detail in your application. You did not put down the date you completed the work of study. Beg your pardon? You did not complete the study. You attended the study. But Miss Jones one of qualifications for this job is the completion of the study. Sorry."

"John and Nancy, I think you are one of the finest young couples I've seen in a long time. I am happy to perform your wedding ceremony. Say, you already have your reservations?" "Going to Atlanta to spent the night and then to Acapulco for a whole week. Reservation's made, tickets ready." "Fantastic! Are you ready to go to the Chapel and we'll have the service and you can be on our way. Oh yes, by the way, I need to see your license? John, you don't look so well. Is there something wrong? No, John, I'm sorry the court house is not open on Saturday. I'm sorry."

My father and I drove to his home together. We knew that he would not be long upon this earth, my paternal grandfather. My father and I wanted to sit up with him on Friday night. It was a very special time. I listened to those two men talk. My father called his father, "Papa." I hope my grandchildren call me, "Papa" They talked all night. Part of the night I was able to sit up. My father never slept a wink that night. He spent the entire night talking to his father. I have looked back on that night many times wishing I had stayed up longer. Why didn't I listen more? Why didn't I just stay up and listen? I spent most of that night sleeping, and look what I missed. Eight days later we stood over his coffin as it was lowered into the ground. That opportunity never came to me again.

They called him "Old Farmer." His name was Alphie Georgeson. He lived in the Willow Bluff Community of Wisconsin. They called him "Old Farmer" because it just seemed to fit. He was an old farmer. That's all he ever wanted to be. He had three changes of clothes: a nice new pair of striped overalls he wore to town and two more faded pairs of overalls in which he worked. His life was centered on the farm. The farm was paid for. It gave to him and Elizabeth a small but adequate income. All of his life he was centered working that farm with Jed and Hank, his favorite horses. Now everyone else used a tractor, but not the "Old Farmer" because he loved those two horses. For twenty years they had been together. A team. They worked together from early of morning to late at night.

Their life was simple and uncomplicated. It was at its best, except for one thing. Elizabeth often wished that Alphie would to go church with her. He talked about it every now and then, but he hadn't been in 50 long years. He knew they would slap him on the back and say, "You rascal, it's about time. I hope the walls don't cave in today because the 'Old Farmer' is here." So he didn't go. He never went to church. There was one time; it was Christmas Eve.

Elizabeth had gone on earlier to practice in the choir before the special service that night. As she came in and occupied the choir loft, she looked out there and there was Alphie. He had with him the five Enderman kids. She thought they had brought him but she found out later it was the other way around. They often came to the house. On that Christmas Eve they seemed to know nothing of the baby Jesus or of Christmas. So Alphie loaded them up in the wagon and brought them to church. But other than that he never went to church. Never. How she wished that he would. How it grieved her so. Every Sunday while she went to church, he would go out to the barn and work and piddle. That's where she found him after church that Sunday. She first thought he was asleep and then she found differently.

The funeral service was nice. They put his coffin in a hay wagon and it was led through the community being drawn by his two prized horses, Jed and Hank. Elizabeth remembered very little of what the preacher said, but she did remember the text he used. "In my Father's house are many mansions: if it were not so, I would have told you. I go to prepare a place for you. And if I go and prepare a place for you, then I will come again, and receive you unto myself; that where I am, there ye may be also, the way ye know."

As she struggled for sleep that night and could not find it, she asked herself. "Did Alphie know the way? Could somehow, in His infinite mercy, Jesus find a place for the "Old Farmer?

The Rich Get Richer
Matthew 25:14-30

THE RICH GET RICHER. Why? He bore the heavy burden of giftedness. He knew everyone knew he was good. His wife 'knew it. His fellow students in the seminary knew it. The professor, Dr. Craddock, who related the story knew it.' The young man knew it, and it scared him to death. He had every gift, every talent, and every ability to be a preacher. It frightened him. After the satisfactory completion of a course of study in seminary, he returned to his home state to his denomination an there received his first church. On the first Sunday he was to give his first sermon, He pulled a George Jones: He didn't show up.

After the special music when it came time for him to preach he was not there. No show! They sang another hymn, nervously counted their shoe laces and kept looking at the empty space behind the pulpit. Still no preacher. His wife was panicky. She ran from the sanctuary, went back to the study and he was not there, She went home and he was not there. She finally found him that afternoon sitting in the park thumbing pebbles in the pond. "What happened?" "I don't know," he said. "Did you have your sermon?" "Yeah, I had my sermon, had it all ready." "What happened?" "I don't know except there was just so much at stake, and I was scared to death. I was afraid."

Is that not what the third servant said? Was that not his excuse for not doing what the master told him to do? "I was frightened. I was scared. There was so much at stake." Now the people who initially heard this story could identify with the third servant very well: The hiding of money in one's back yard (in a fruit jar?) was a common practice. There were no FDIC, no governmental bailout, and no guarantees! We're talking about the investment of money. We're not talking about gifts. We're not talking about talents. The original context of Jesus' Word here is talking about the investment of money. The man was afraid. So frightened was he that he hid the money and did nothing with it. A good conservative philosophy. It could have been worse. He could have lost it. Instead he didn't lose it. He just did nothing with it. When the master returned he gave him what he had originally received. Can you identify with that? I can.

My father was a child of the depression, and all of my life I have been taught the conservative philosophy of money. My father used to tell me, "Son, save ten percent of everything you make." How I wish I had listened to my father. How I wish I could have saved ten percent of everything I make. I was told certain things like; if in doubt take the old and proven path. A bird in hand is worth two in the bush. Rather be safe than sorry. Be conservative; that is a wise counsel and a good philosophy. But is there more? Is there another way? Is that always in every case wise counsel and wisdom?

My good friend, Tommy Garrison, a pastor here in our city, tells the story about a grocer. The grocer is starting his own business. He goes into it with mixed emotions and says to himself, "This may not work. It might fail." With that as his premise, he enters this enterprise. Instead of getting a nice, prominent building, well located, well lit, he rents on the back street a little dingy building where the rent is cheap. Instead of obtaining one of the nice cash registers that helps, he keep up with the inventory in a cigar box. Instead of hiring nice good capable help, he manage it most of the time, and every now and then a relative will come in and sort of help out when he's not there.

Instead of having real nice attractive produce, he has dark bananas, wrinkled oranges, and less than yellow lemons, etc. Instead of having a real nice expensive sign, hanging out on the front, he paints a little piece of cardboard with crayons. "No one really spends a lot of money on advertising these days. Besides they know where the grocery is anyway." Instead of having a nice parking lot where people can conveniently park and get in and out of the rain and bad weather, he provided none of that. "You know the walk will do them good." Of course, the enterprise fails. Then he goes to his family and says, "Family, congratulate me. I'm a wise man. See how much money I could have lost? Was that wise? Was that a good philosophy of the investment of money?

Why was the master so harsh upon the third servant? Why did he demand so much more? Possibly because the servant had so much more to give. A talent in money was worth as much as $30,000.00 in our money and some say even as high as the equivalent to three years of labor. Five, two or one, it was still a lot of money. The master demanded of the servant his very best use of the creativity and ingenuity that had been entrusted to him. But instead he panicked, paralyzed in fear of embarrassment, of failure, of loss, of punishment, but, basically, he was afraid to risk.

That is not only true in business, it is true in our personal faith and in the functioning of a church as well. We cannot be the personal servant and we can't be the servant church unless we are willing to risk. We cannot care for people unless we are willing TO risk. We cannot give of our money unless we are willing to risk. We cannot love people unless we are willing to risk. We cannot witness to people unless we are willing to risk. We cannot have faith, hope, we cannot do anything as a servant of God, either, as a person, or as a church unless we are willing to risk. It is at the point of need, we find the point of risk. Unless we are willing to risk, we will not be able to meet the need.

One of the most perfect examples of that is a hug. A hug! To hug someone, to embrace someone, to accept someone through a hug, we first have to let down our defenses. Then we must throw open our arms, and in doing so we run the risk of being vulnerable. We are vulnerable to them where they can hit us in the heart or they can accept us with a hug in return.

Do you remember the parable Jesus told of the shepherd? The shepherd has ninety-nine sheep, but one is lost and the shepherd leaves the ninety and nine and goes to look for the one lost sheep. Now Matthew and Luke both tell the story. Matthew tells it this way: The shepherd leaves ninety and nine and goes to look for the one, leaving the ninety and nine in the fold. IF he finds that one there will be rejoicing.

Luke tells the story differently. Luke tells the story this way that the shepherd leaves the ninety and nine in the desert running loose and goes and searches for the lost sheep until he finds it. Do you hear the risk in that? He leaves the ninety arid nine running loose and searches for the lost sheep until he finds it. There is a shepherd who is willing to risk the welfare of the ninety and nine. He is willing to risk his own welfare to go and find the lost sheep. This is a shepherd who says, "Whatever it takes. Whatever it takes I will find the sheep."

The church says, "Whatever it takes we will reach people for the Lord Jesus Christ." Whatever it takes. Why does the shepherd leave the ninety and nine running loose and searches until he finds the lost sheep? Only one reason. LOVE! He loves the sheep. Why are we willing to take the risk? Because of love. What was Jesus' motivating factor to leave the glories of heaven and come upon this earth arid live as we live, to suffer as we suffer, to "be tempted as we are tempted, to walk in the steps in which we walk; to suffer the pain and humiliation of the cross? Did He have in His pocket a written guarantee that everything would be fine and dandy? NO! He did it just like we do it - on faith. FAITH! He was willing to risk it all because he could trust the Father. He calls us to do the same. Are we willing to risk, to take a stand to be God's people, to be the servant we can be personally and to be the servant we can be as a church?   This is the question that is before us. This is a question we need to consider as the Vision '90 Committee is at work setting long range plans as to where this church is going in the next ten years.

Twenty-five years ago a group of, people built this building, and doing so took a risk. They "faithed it" for people who were not even born yet - for people whose parents were not even yet born. They took a chance and, for the past twenty-five years that same group of people have been doing, the same. Now the question comes to us: Is it now our time? Are we willing to do the same? We know that cannot grow tomorrow's church totally dependent upon yesterday's resources. It will not work. It didn't work for the grocer. It won't work in your automobile. It won't work in your computer. It won't work in your business. It won't work in your home, and it won't work in the church. We cannot grow tomorrow's church totally, completely one-hundred percent dependent on yesterday's resources. It means we have to risk. We have to see beyond our generation to the next generation and to the next generation.

"Prove the Tithe Day" is not just proving to God, but proving to ourselves what we can do it if we are willing to risk and exercise faith. To reach people, we must provide a new roof for this building, an elevator, a new educational structure, re-light the sanctuary, re-sound the sanctuary, re-do the third floor, payoff our fellowship hall, and buy a new bus. We need to provide resources that God can use to grow His church. Two-thousand by 2000 is not just a catchy phrase. It is a realistic possibility. It is a potential that we can reach if we are willing to work, to pray and be God's people. Ten years from now we can stand in this very same pulpit, in this very same building with one thousand people in Sunday School if we are willing to pay the price, to risk, and to be God's people.

Jesus used an illustration in the Sermon on the Mount about a lamp. He said, "You are the lamp. You are that light. You don't put a light under a bushel" Now, why would anyone put a light under a bushel? Well, it's simple; to keep the candle from going out. You put a light under a bushel because we are afraid it's going to go out: But this is the purpose of the church. It is not our job to keep the light going. That's God's business. It is our purpose to take the light into darkness. It is our purpose to take the bushel off and to go out into the darkness, and light up the dark places with the light of Jesus' love so that the Father in heaven might be glorified. That's our purpose. It will happen if we're willing to risk, to take a step, to go forward in faith.

You remember my preacher buddy I talked about in the beginning of the sermon? "George Jones." Well, the church board met and gave him another chance. "No games," they said, "you've got one more chance." The next Sunday when it came time to preach, he was there. As soon as the services were dismissed he went to his study and wrote a note to his professor. It had

1:15 pm on it. These were the words that he wrote: "Dear Prof, Today I dropped a pebble into the pond. Whether or not it causes ripples' or whether or not they reach the shore. It yet remains to be seen."

Whether it causes a ripple or whether they reach the shore, it yet remains to be seen. It yet remains to be seen what First Baptist People can do if we're willing to work, to pray, to risk, to take a chance for our Lord. It remains to be seen.

What are You Doing with What You've Got?
Matthew 25:14-30

A young sailor in World II was reading a book in his local library when he noticed some margin notations that were made by a female hand. Instead of reading the book, he started reading the notations. They were beautifully written, deeply warm and sensitive, and you might even call them spiritual. He was so impressed that he asked the librarian the name of the young lady who wrote them. He got her name and sent an introductory letter to the address which at that time was called overseas. Once overseas they began corresponding with each other. They corresponded for over a year, and their relationship deepened. He continued to be impressed by her wit, charm, personality and, yes, her spirituality. He sent her a picture of himself, but she did not sent him a picture of herself.

When he returned to the States, they decided they would meet at Grand Central Station on a certain day at 7:00 o'clock. He would know her, having never seen her, by a red rose in her lapel. At 7:00 o'clock, all of a sudden one of the most beautiful and attractive women he had ever seen in all of his life started toward him. His heart leaped up into his throat and he thought, "Oh, could she be the one?" He looked and there was no rose in her lapel.

As she walked past him, she said, "Sailor, going my way?" As he looked past her, there was the one wearing a rose in her lapel. His countenance fell, disappointment reigned and he was almost tempted to go after the tall, attractive lady who had just passed in the pale green suit. But he thought, "No, there is the one with the rose in her lapel, twice his age, graying, plain and round. He turned his back on the beautiful woman in the pale green suit and went to his friend. He took her by the hand, introduced himself, kissed her hand and said, "Would you please join me for dinner tonight?" The lady responded, "Son, I don't know what is going on, but that very attractive lady in the pale green suit that just walked past you, begged me to wear this rose. She said that if you asked me out to dinner, she would be in the restaurant across the street. She said it was something about a test."

We don't like tests, do we? Tests make us discover some things about ourselves. We discover what we think about ourselves: We discover what we think about others. And sometimes we even discover what we think about God. To take a test is to take a risk. Tests give 'F's" as well as "A's". You not only can excel on the test, but you can fail as well. Sometimes we lose a lot if we fail.

In 1932, a traveler beaten down by the weather, half- starving, thirsting to death in the desert wandered upon an old well. Attached to the well was a note that read, "This well has never run dry. There is water for all. Only the leather washer gets dried out and the pump needs to be primed. West from the well you will find a rock and under the rock you will find a bottle of water corked. Take one-half of the water, pour it down the well, moisten the washer and then pour the rest down the well. Pump like crazy, and you will have all the water you need. Do not drink the water that's in the bottle. Pour it all down the well. Have faith. Your friend, Cactus Pete."

Could you trust Cactus Pete? Could you take the only bottle of water that might save your life and pour it down the well, lose it all in an effort to gain enough for yourself and others? It is a risk.

The Bible is full of people who took risks. Think of the risk that Abraham and Sarah took when he left all and went to the land that God had promised to him. Think of David, the shepherd boy, as he stood before Goliath. Think of the risk that Moses took as he went back to Egypt when he was wanted there for murder. Think of the risk that Joseph took when he believed the dream that his wife, now pregnant, was a virgin. And think of Mary and the risk that she took from a heavenly voice that said she would be the mother of the Messiah. She risked her reputation and her very life. And think of the risk that Jesus took when He willingly, without offering resistance though powerful He was, allowed Himself to be crucified in faith, risking that God would raise Him from the dead.

The Bible is full of people who took risks for God. Is there anything or anyone for whom you would risk anything or everything? Jesus told a story about a master - this is not a God figure but a shrewd business man who risked a lot with three servants. To one he gave five talents of money, an enormous sum. To another he gave two talents, still an enormous sum, and to another he gave one talent, which probably is equal to a quarter of a million dollars in our language. One made five more and brought it back, one made two more and brought it back; but the one with only one talent did nothing. When he brought it back, it was taken from him. Verse 29 becomes the key verse in understanding the parable when Jesus said, "That which you have will be taken from you unless you use it." Either use it or lose it! It's a warning, if you will, that if we don't use our talents, gifts and abilities and assume responsibility, they will be taken from us.

Frank Pollard tells the story of several years ago when an individual died and his will left his farm to Satan. Literally left his farm to Satan! The courts did not know what to do. How do you give a farm to Satan? They decided they would do nothing. No one broke the ground, no one sowed the seed, no one tended the fences, no one tended the barns, no one tended the animals and through negligence, the farm literally went to the Devil.

How is it that we can let things go to Satan? We might respond, "But I don't have anything. I don't have any abilities or gifts or talents or resources, but the Bible says that is not so. God will never call you to do anything that He does not equip you to do.

In our text for today, the one who had only one talent still had a tremendous amount of money to be put into the hand of a slave. Can you imagine how much freedom that gave him? Which one of these do you identify with? It is hard to identify with the fellow who had five talents, a million and a quarter. If you are like me -- and we have some five talent people in our congregation and on our staff -- but most of us have two talents or maybe just one talent What we have, whether it be one talent or two or if you are gifted enough to have five, that is what God will require of you, and that is enough to do anything God would have you to do. God will never call you to do anything He does not equip you to do; and that gives us a marvelous, wonderful freedom to accept the responsibility that God has placed upon us.

Then to attempt even the small things we do in life risk is involved. The risk to witness is the risk of being laughed about the risk of trust is the risk of being betrayed. The risk of loving is the risk that we will be rejected. The risk of giving to God financially is the risk that we won't have everything we think we need for ourselves. You see, the everyday experiences of hope and belief and trust and giving and loving and caring as a Christian all require risk. The church - what a risk we took in adopting the greatest and largest budget in our history. What a risk the church took in opening the School of Fine Arts. What a risk we're taking as we're seeking to open a Christian Counseling Center. What a risk we will take if we reach out in faith to unchurched people. The Christian life is full of risk. Not only is the Bible full of risk, so is the church of today and so is our church. Never let it be said by any of us that we don't have what is necessary to achieve what God is leading us to do.

As the poet said, "It's not what you do with riches if millions should be your lot, but what are you doing today with the buck thirty-five you've got?" That is the question! It's not what we would do if we all have, the question is, and what are we doing today with what we have – one talent, two talents or five talents? We might answer, "I'm afraid." That's what the servant said. To be honest with you, I can identify with him. It is a scary thing to have something that God has entrusted to us, to have a responsibility to God and have gifts or talents or resources or abilities that God can use. That is an awesome responsibility. It's scary! Sometimes we are scared to death that God might do something.

It's a true story. A preacher went to a nursing home to visit one of his parishioners. She had been in the nursing home for several months and was having trouble with her legs. They had a nice visit and she asked the preacher to have prayer with her. He said, "Of course, I would be glad to." He had prayer with her. He prayed for her healing and as soon as the prayer was over, she looked at him and said, "Pastor!" She grabbed him by the shoulder, sat up on the side of the bed, stood up in the room, began to walk around the room, and said, "I'm healed!" The preacher turned every color in the book, got out of that room as fast as he could, ran to his car, sat down behind the steering wheel and said, "Lord, don't you ever do that to me again!" It's a scary thing! It's a frightening thing that God would actually work through us, but He will. Sometimes we are afraid that God will do something, but most of the time we're afraid that he won't, or we are afraid that we can't; and we take our talents, our abilities and our resources and we bury them.

They said that it actually happened a few years ago in Houston, Texas. A mistake was made and a two year old child was summoned for jury duty. It is sort of ironic, isn't it? The children really are our judge and jury. Our children, the next generation, really are our judge and jury of the decisions we make, of the choices we make, and the way we utilize what God has given to us. Children are really our judge as to what we have done with what we've got and what we have left to them.

His name was Hans Bablinger. Hans lived in Ulm, Germany. He was a dreamer, a risk taker. Hans wanted to fly. He wanted to soar like an eagle. There's only one thing wrong, Hans lived in the 16th Century, and they didn't have airplanes or helicopters or anything like that in those days. But still he wanted to fly, and he was not afraid to take the risk. His business was making artificial limbs, and he made himself some wings. He went to a certain place in the Bavarian Alps, got in a good undercurrent and leaped off. For a short period of time Hans flew and came to a safe landing on the ground. The people cheered. Hans was elated and God rejoiced. (I think God likes risk takers.)

Hans's fame spread far and near. The king heard about Hans and was invited by the local bishop to come to the sanctuary in Ulm. The bishop wanted Hans to show off for the king. They didn't go up into the Alps as once they had. It would be easier for everybody and especially the king if they stayed on flat land. Bad choice! So when Hans tried to fly again, you can guess what happened. He sank like a rock in the river. Defeated, the next Sunday the preacher's sermon was entitled, "Man Was Not Meant to Fly." Hans was defeated, his spirit crushed, and he was embarrassed publicly. Hans never tried to fly again. Not the first time nor the last that the pulpit has tried to tell someone what they could not do. Hans died very shortly thereafter, a very defeated man Oh, yes, and the church at Ulm, guess what, it's empty. The only people who go to that church are tourists. How did the tourists get to Ulm? You guessed it. They flew.

Who Takes the Responsibility?
Matthew 25: 14-30

What I want to talk with you about this morning is, who takes the responsibility? That's a big word -- "responsibility." As I was preparing for this message, I could not help but harken back to days of yore when I was a senior in high school. Everyone was excited about our football team. This was to be the "Year of the Lion" -- the Sardis Lions. We had the best center in the state at 5 ft. 10 in., 215 pounds -- he was "first team - All State." Our quarterback and our fullback both later signed with Auburn. Our line was two-deep in every position. We had lettermen at every position. Everyone was filled with excitement -- THIS COULD BE OUR YEAR, but it wasn't!

I have thought many times, how could a team so filled with potential, a great coaching staff, with that weight, speed, and experience NOT make it? We did play the most difficult schedule that the school has ever played. We finished with five wins, three losses and two ties. It was not a happy year for anyone. I have wondered often, why? My conclusion is this -- we didn't have leadership. We had a tremendous amount of potential, unlimited talent, size, and speed; but yet within that group of young men, there was no one, NO ONE, including me, came to the forefront and said. "I am going to be the leader. I am going to be the one who takes responsibility.

Julius Irving, "Doctor J" as he is best known, has been one of the great class acts in basketball and humanity, He has not only been a great ball player, but he has been a great individual. He has been a fine Christian, giving many, many hours to public service. He is retiring this year, and public life and basketball will miss "Doctor J."

I heard him interviewed not long ago as he was talking about the future of the Philadelphia 76ers, the team for which he plays. He made this statement in talking about a promising player on the team by the name of Charles Barkley. He said, "Barkley will have to do one thing. He will have to make up his mind to be the leader of the team." Everyone knew that had been the position assumed by Doctor J. Now he said, "Barkley will have to make up his mind that he is going to take the responsibility of whether this team wins or loses."

He was saying that someone has to take the responsibility. Someone has to say, "The buck stops here." If you will look over your sports history, every great team has had at least one of those individuals - a John Havlicek, or Larry Byrd, or Dale Murphy, LeBron James or Nancy Leiberman, or some individual who says, "When it comes down to it, when the chips are down, you can depend on me. When the game is on the line, I WANT THE BALL! I want the responsibility as to whether we "win or lose."

The same is true not only in sports but in life. Someone in the family has to say. "I am going to take the responsibility of whether this is a successful family. It won't just happen! Someone has to say. "I take the responsibility. I will be responsible as to whether this family succeeds or not. It is the same in our families, in sports, in business, and it is the same in the church. Every successful church has people within it who say, "I am going to take the responsibility of whether God's work flourishes here or not. I am going to take the responsibility. The buck stops here. It depends on me. I am not going to be satisfied to just let it go, just let it happen if it will. No, I am going to make it happen. I am going to take the responsibility. I am going to fulfill my place of leadership.

I really think that is the attitude in which Jesus tells one of his most famous parables, the parable of the talents. The story is one very familiar to you, and I will go through it just briefly again. It is a story of a man who had great wealth. A talent was a large sum of money in those days. He was going on a journey and he gathered three his servants. He said, "I am going to give each of you responsibility.

Some of you are going to have more than the others, but all of you are going to have some responsibility according to your ability, and he did. Five talents, two talents, and one talent he gives to them. The man with five talents said initially, "Now what am I going to do with this investment? I can sit back. I can hide it, or I can go to work and take responsibility for it." The Bible says he doubled it. The same thing happened with the servant who had two. When the master comes back, he rewards both of them equally. He did not reward success, he rewarded faithfulness. He rewarded the one with five talents and the one with two talents equally.

The main character in the story, of course, is the man with one talent, who refused to do something with it. The emphasis of the story is really upon him. He did not do anything; his goal was no goal, and he did nothing. When he returned the servant was accountable to the master. He asked him what he had done. He responded out of fear, "Oh, I was afraid and so I did nothing. Here is your one talent." Then Jesus says, "The master called him a "wicked servant." This is one the harshest words in the entire Bible -- used sixteen times. Ten of those times this word is used to refer to Satan. It is a harsh, severe word that he called the servant, not because of what he did but because of what he did not do.

"You are wicked," he said, "because you have done nothing. Therefore, that which you have will be taken away from you and it will be given to someone I can trust to be responsible." What does this mean? What does this say to you and me?

I think first of all it says that God needs us. That initially sounds blasphemous to say that God needs us. God doesn't really need anything. He has everything, so why does God need us? Well, God has chosen to do certain things and allow you and me to cooperate with Him in their accomplishment. God could do everything, and we know that; but He has chosen to use us in places of responsible leadership to be his co-partner. If we are to be His joint heir up there, why should we not be His co-partner down here? So God needs us to the extent that He has chosen to give us the responsibility to be His co-partner and when we cooperate with Him, we serve Him. When we do nothing. We cooperate with someone else.

Frank Pollard reminds us of the true story of a farmer of disreputable character who willed his farm to Satan. The courts didn't know what to do, uh, where are you going to deliver the deed? Where does Satan live? I have never met him, but I think I've known some of his relatives. What are you going to do with this, for that belongs to Satan? You know what they did? They did nothing. They didn't till the soil, they didn't fertilize the land, they didn't irrigate, they didn't sow, they didn't reap -- THEY DIDN'T DO ANYTHING!

They felt to do nothing was the best way they could fulfill the family's wishes of willing his farm to Satan. You don't have to do anything to ruin your family. You don't have to come home drunk and beat your family to ruin it -- just do nothing. Don't love them, don't encourage them. You don't have to hold your children down and shoot dope into their arms to ruin them -- don't love them, don't care about them. You don't have to go out and rob your company blind to ruin it - just don't do anything -- don't care -- don't go to work -- don't be faithful -- don't take responsibility. You don't have to get on the streets and march in front of our church and use slanderous gossip against it to ruin it. Just do nothing! Don't attend, don't give, don't love, and don't serve, don't be responsible -- just do nothing! When we cease to cooperate with God, we begin to cooperate with somebody else. The unpardonable sin that the Bible talks about is really a result of doing nothing. We do nothing for so long until we get to the point where we can't do anything. That's the unpardonable sin. We fail to listen to God so long until we get to the point that we cannot hear him. That's the unpardonable sin. It begins by doing nothing!

The servant was called "wicked" and began that road to being called "wicked" the minute he said his talent was not needed. God needs each of us. God needs every one of us. We are all needed by God and have the wondrous privilege of cooperating with Him to accomplish His purposes.

The parable also tells us that God needs each of us. He not only needs us, but he needs each of us and what we have. Jesus is very realistic here. He is saying that not everyone is equally gifted in talents and ability -- some have five; some have two; and some of us have one. But we all have at least one. We all have something we can do for our Lord. There is a place of responsibility for each and every one of us. The little poem says,

> It is not what you would do with millions if riches should be your lot.
> What are you doing today with the buck thirty-five you've got?

Rockefeller did have millions, but there was a time he made $4.35 a week, and he tithed that! God needs each of us. He needs the talent you have. He needs the gifts you have. He needs the money you have. He needs the responsibility you can assume. He needs each of us, and He needs what we have to give to fulfill our particular place and responsibility in His kingdom. The Bible not only says that God needs each of us; but it says that our responsibility begins with a definite commitment. I think the three servants first sat down and said, "What am I going to do? What is my plan, my goal, my ambition? What am I going to do with that which the master has entrusted to me?" One no doubt said, "I am going to work." The second one said "I am going to work." The third said, "I am just not going to do anything. Every result was an outcome of a definite commitment and intention on the part of the person.

What kind of goal, what kind of ambition do we have for ourselves and for our church? He is calling upon us to become responsible. He is calling upon us to set a goal and to assume our place of responsibility.

Just not long ago I began to look at my own personal finances, and I began to look at my own pattern of giving. I said, "If I am to fulfill my goal of tithing this year, I've got to start giving more money the last nine months than I gave in the first three months." I set my goal of giving $15.00 a week more the last nine months than I gave in the first three. It won't just happen! We have to set a definite goal and assume a responsibility to achieve that goal.

Possibly some of you need to do the same. Our giving records would indicate that. Right now at this we are giving about 85% of our budget. That will not make it. Our church has a history in that we make up the deficit at the year. We went into the last month of December last year with a budget deficit-- had a great ingathering of funds, and everyone rejoiced. We cannot rest on those laurels. Yesterday's success will not fill today's responsibility and will not pave the future for God's work to be done. We cannot wait until the end of the year and have to raise a quarter of a million dollars. Someone, many of us, are going to have to stop right now and look into our hearts, our own patterns of giving, and say, who is going to take the responsibility?" "Am I going to take responsibility? Yes, I am going to take responsibility! I am going to make up my mind! I am going to have a definite role to play in whether God's work flourishes or not at First Baptist Church. If we takes responsibility? We do! We have to!"

People are always trying to categorize sins. When I was growing up, people categorized sins. A lot of people were interested in that sort of thing and tried to decide which the worst sins were and which were the least sins. Usually the sins people thought were the worst were the sins they were not committing! A lot of people were interested in that kind of thing; and they would tell us teenaged boys and girls what were the worst sins and what were not the worst sins. Believe it or not, in those days, one of the worst sins perceived by many was that of dancing. Dancing! They were afraid that boys and girls would touch each other! It might not be a problem today. Today one gets over here and one gets over there, and they each have a fit in their own place. So it might not be the problem today as it was then! They hardly see each other, much less touch! In those days, it was. I didn't know that. I guess my education was deficient. I was a member of a small dance band in an effort to make my spending money. We played for proms and sock hops.

On Saturdays I worked on a milk truck. The driver would pick me up about 7:00 in the morning, and I would help him deliver milk. One night we played very late on the other end of the county, and I was 5:00 AM getting home. I was dead tired from having worked all night. When the milkman came by to get me to work the next morning, I told Mother. "I'm just too tired; I've only had two hours of sleep. I believe I'll just sleep in today." About thirty minutes later my Dad came into the room. "Son, what are you doing?" "I'm sleeping, Dad; I worked all night." He said, "Aren't you supposed to be on the milk truck?" I said, "Yes sir, but I didn't get but two hours of sleep." He said. "Get your clothes on." I said, "What?" He said, "Get your clothes on. We are going to find Jack, and you are going to work." I will never forget what he said.

"Son it's simple. When you take a job, you do it. When you take a responsibility, you do it. Period." I have never forgotten that.

It may be difficult; it may be hard. It may require more of us than we think we've got to give, but what is the alternative? Do nothing! Shirk responsibility. I had rather work hard and give it all I've got and more to have the Master say, "Welcome, thou good and faithful servant. You've been faithful over a few things. I will make you ruler over many," than for the Master to come and look at me, "Why did you do NOTHING?" Pray tell me, please pray tell me, as we stand before Jesus with the nail prints in His hands and in His feet. What excuse could we give for doing nothing?

When Judgment is Good
Matthew 25:31-46

Here ye! Here ye! The court now is in session. The Honorable Judge says, "Please rise." With that statement, the defendant rises from his table. He takes one glance at the front of the courtroom. He begins to rub his eyes because he just simply cannot believe, what he is seeing. His mind races back to the evening before when he and his wife were dining in their favorite restaurant at their favorite table. It was the one by the window, but he did not mind so much looking upon the city because it gave him energy and vitality. He was at his usual table by the window, not celebrating so much with his wife, but trying to escape just a little because he was anxious about the court appearance in the morning. And as they are sharing time together and he is cutting into his favorite fillet, there is a beggar staring at him in the window. It is a dirty beggar; obviously a homeless person with long stringy black hair and dirty clothes. He can almost smell him through the window. He is not a pretty sight with scars all over his face. It is a disturbing sight and the man asked the waiter, "Will you please tell that man to leave? I cannot eat my meal in peace."

And lo, and behold, as he looked at the judge upon the bench, it is the same face. The same face! The very same face that he saw in the hungry homeless beggar the night before as he dined upon fillet mignon was now looking at him from the bench. The very same face stares at him. The beggar who would have the crumbs from his table only the night before, is now the one who sits upon the bench in judgment of the defendant. It was C. S. Lewis who said, "When the author comes upon the stage the play is over." Well, folks the play is over.

When we get to this point in the Gospel of Matthew, everything Matthew has been trying to say is now summarized in this parable. It's over! History is over! Opportunity is over and now the Son of Man comes in his glory. The very same Son of Man! Yes! Jesus himself. Jesus who had no place to lay His head while upon earth, now sits upon a royal throne. The very same Jesus who had no home and was even rejected by the people in His own hometown, now sits in judgment upon all of the families of the earth. The very same Jesus, who was accused of being in a league with Satan, now sits as the judge over Satan and every one of his evil works. The very same Jesus who was challenged by Satan to "throw yourself down from the temple," now sits over all the temples of all the world and His angels reign with Him. The very same Jesus who was killed at the hands of hateful men now is raised again and sits in loving judgment over all people. And everyone is there. All nations and all people are there. Every person who ever drew breath upon this planet now sits before Jesus, and He is the judge. His criteria for judgment have not changed. It is standard. It has been written since the foundation of the world. It is not there to be criticized. It is only to be accepted and to be answered. His criteria for judgment is simple. It is one statement. It is not up for judgment, we are!

A man once went to one of the great national art galleries and looked at some of the pictures and said, "I don't like those pictures." The attendant just happened to be standing by and said, "Sir, the pictures are not on trial." Jesus standard of judgment is not on trial; we are. His standard of judgment is very, very simple. It is one statement - how have you responded to human need?

How have you served your neighbor? It is just that simple. It is not easy, but it is just that simple. How have you responded? How have you served those that have been put before you in need? How have you responded to those who rejoice, those for whom judgment is good, and for those who receive their inheritance? They did so in little simple acts of kindness. They did so in simple deeds that anyone can do. They fed the hungry. They gave the thirsty something to drink. They visited those who were in prison. They clothed those who needed clothing. They provided homes for those who needed homes; they went and visited the sick and supplied prayer and encouragement. Little simple acts! Acts that we saw reproduced here in this congregation of faith and throughout our entire city yesterday through Operation Inasmuch. People! Dozens upon dozens with different tasks simply trying to share Christ love in concrete ways, in. Simple acts of kindness that any individual could do. That is all it takes. In uncalculating ways. Some were planned, I'm sure. Some were spontaneous, I'm sure. But all were done in uncalculating ways, never trying to earn one measure of God's grace and love, but to simply return to him out of the grace and love that already we have known. Then the most marvelous thing happened. Not only were these simple acts of kindness that anyone can do, done in uncalculating and non-devious ways but then the marvelous surprise came. The wonderful surprise is that in doing these simple acts to those in need we are actually doing it to Jesus, Himself.

The very face of Jesus was seen in countless individuals all throughout Chattanooga yesterday as this church went out and blanketed this city with the love of Christ. What a marvelous, wonderful surprise we could actually be doing something for our Lord. I thought that if Jesus had to come back yesterday, a lot of people would be very, very happy because they were already answering the final exam. They were already preparing for his coming by doing those simple acts of kindness.

I remember when I was a sophomore in college, I was taking a zoology course and the professor right before the final exam, gave us a study sheet. He said, "Work on that study sheet and you will be fine." I worked myself to death on that study sheet. I filled out every question in minute detail and did my best to memorize it. Low and behold I received the most wonderful surprise when I went in to take the final exam. The professor passed out the final exam and it was exactly the same as the study sheet. How good it is to take an exam when you already know the question.

God's final exam you already know! There is only one question upon it. How have you responded to human need in the name of the Lord Jesus Christ? It is a happy time. I made an "A' believe it or not. It is a happy time when you can pass the exam with flying colors, when you knew the questions ahead of time and you gave your time and energy to do so. We hear those marvelous words "Come, good and faithful servants. Receive your inheritance. Welcome to the joys of your Lord." Could there be any greater joy than going out in the name of Jesus knowing his love and power is going with you, spreading that loving power to others and looking upon their face and seeing the face of Jesus reflected back to you. Could there be greater joy? Could there be more happiness.

Gettis McGregory tells the story of when he was a five year old little boy overhearing a conversation between his aunt and uncle and his parents. The aunt and uncle said, "We are so glad you chose to have little Gettis. He is such a source of joy to us." Gettis said, "I thought about that at five and I have thought about it many times since and it dawned upon me that someone actually made a decision for me to be here. I am here and I would not be here if they had not, but I am here because someone made a decision for me to be here." And from that he concluded what the Bible says over and over again that life is a gift. Every talent that we have, every dollar that we have, even the very breath that we breathe is a gift from God. Life, itself, is a gift from God. We are here because God made a decision for us to be here. And the very life we live we give back to Him in service to the one who gave it to us in the beginning.

Operation Inasmuch! "For in as much as you have done it unto the least of these, you have done it unto me." Could there be greater joy? Could there be more than being on mission for Christ?

It was 1933 when this uncanonized saint of the homeless printed the first copy of the Catholic Worker. She sold it, I think, for a penny, but it might have been a nickel. She printed two hundred and fifty copies. Within two years they had a circulation of one hundred and fifty thousand. Harvey Cox, America's greatest theologian, has called her the greatest Catholic theologian of the twentieth century. Her name was Dorothy Day. She started her little newspaper, which caught on like wildfire, but then she opened her first house of hospitality when a woman read her newspaper and asked her if she could do something for her. In other words put some action behind your words. Dorothy Day did just that. She took the woman into her own little skimpy apartment. Now the Catholic Worker movement has over one hundred and seventy five homes for the homeless throughout the United States and the world. This was made possible because of one woman. One woman who decided to not just talk about her faith, which she did so eloquently, but lived it as well said, "It is the child of God who sees Christ in the face of the poor."

My favorite story about her is this. A writer of the New York Times went to interview Dorothy Day. He went to one of her houses of hospitality where she lived and out of which she worked. He came upon her and she was in conversation with a homeless person. She kept talking to that person for five, ten, fifteen, twenty minutes. The city writer was getting a little bit irritated that he was being ignored and in his own self-importance he finally cleared his throat so many times, she had to notice him: And then she hurried to him and said, "Oh, I'm sorry: Did you wish to speak to one of us."

Sometimes You Never Know!
Matthew 25:31-46

You know, sometimes you never know! You never know! John Blanchard tells this story about himself. When he was in a library in Florida he came upon a book and in the margin of the book there were some notations of a very special nature of kindness and generosity. He tried to track down the individual who wrote them and he did. He found out after much searching that her name was Miss Hollis Maynell and she lived in New York City.

He wrote a letter introducing himself to her and they began a correspondence right after he was transferred overseas during World War II. During the thirteen months that he was overseas they corresponded frequently. A relationship began to flourish and they decided that when he came back to the United States they would get together.

Often times he would ask her for a photograph and she would refuse. She said, "If you care, the photograph would not really matter." So it was on this day in Grand Central station at seven p.m. he was to meet Miss Hollis Maynell. She told him he would recognize her by the red rose that she wore in her lapel and she would recognize him by that same book which he still clutched in his hand. He waited and he waited. He stood and straightened his army uniform because she would be coming very soon and he would see her. Then she came, a beautiful woman – a tall, slender, beautiful blond hair, with a face that shown brightness, a face that was kind and loving, a face that said in his own heart that she lit up the springtime. But then he noticed that this beautiful woman in the light green dress was not wearing a rose in her lapel. He saw her and his heart went out to her. If only that would be her and then she passed him by and as she did she said, "Going my way, Sailor?"

And then he looked over her shoulder and saw Miss Hollis Maynell. There she stood with the rose in her lapel, with her hair bundled up under her hat, well past forty, well past being plump, but yet her face was kind and her heart he knew. He knew not her face, but he knew her heart and he said to himself that this can never be the love that I once envisioned, but she can be my friend. I am going to her. So he straightened up his uniform and saluted. He then walked up to her and said, "My name is Lt. John Blanchard. You must be Miss Hollis Maynell. Would you have dinner with me tonight?"

He was hoping that his disappointment was not evident in his words. Then she responded, "Son, I don't know what is going on here. That women who just passed you in the light green suit begged me to wear this flower. She said that if you came up to me and asked me to dinner, then she would be waiting for you in the big restaurant across the street. She said something about it being some kind of test. You never know! Sometimes you never know!

You never know that each and every day is a test, because some fail and some win in life. Some fail and some win at life! There are some winners and some losers. The Bible says that there will come a day when there will be the ultimate test, the final test, when Jesus himself will set in judgment on each and every one of us and there will be some on the right hand and some on the left hand. There will be the good on the right and the evil on the left; the sheep on the right and the goats on the left. Jesus, himself, will make the judgment. You never know! Sometimes you never know!

Each and every single day is a test. As those days add up to weeks and months, they become the experience that dictates whether we win or lose in this life and whether we win or lose in life to come. You never know what a day might bring. Who knows what even this day might bring. You know Abraham was just sitting there in the middle of the daytime just sorta lollygagging around the encampment when all of a sudden three individuals came up. Immediately he sensed something in his heart. He sensed that it was special and he entertained angels unawares. Then you know one of those angels spoke and one of those voices was the voice of God.

Mary was just going to anoint a body. What could be more morbid and mundane than that - to anoint a body? And then she was the first witness to an event that had never happened before and yet to happen since. She was the first to witness an event that changed her life, and changed the life of the world. She saw Jesus, the resurrected Christ, the Lord of Lords and King of Kings. You never know! You never know what a small act of kindness can have big eternal consequences. We are talking about a Matthew 25 Drive of bringing food, clothes, and things to minister to others just as Christ commanded us to do in the parable. Who knows what God can do as he takes that and magnifies that to encourage and help others. Who knows what small act of kindness we do, God will take and magnify far beyond our imagination.

She was a complainer. She was a self-devoured complainer. She said she complained about everything. She became converted to Christ. She complained about everything. She said she complained that we treat our very Bibles better than we treat the poor. So she began to try to do something and began writing a newspaper that listed her complaints. A woman read the newspaper and came to her apartment and said, "I do not have a home. I am homeless." And Dorothy Day in May of 1933 invited that woman into her home and began the Catholic Worker Movement. She began the movement that now has over one hundred and seventy-five homes for the homeless all over the world.

Tens of thousands have been given homes. Millions have been fed and it began with one woman inviting a homeless woman into her home. Who knows that God can take such a little and insignificant act and magnify it many, many times over. You never know! You never know!! You never know what one day will bring. You never know what one person can become.

There is an old tale told of a German schoolmaster who everyday would go and bow down before the students in his class. He did it every single day and someone asked him, "Why are you doing this? Why is a schoolmaster bowing before his students?" He said, "You never know! You never know who or what one of these students might become." One of those students was a young man by the name of Martin Luther. You never know! You never know what a day might bring. You never know what that person with whom you have influenced might become.

He was a five year old black boy in South Africa in the days of apartheid. Those were the days of racial hatred, bigotry and prejudice. One day he was walking down the street on the sidewalk with his mother. In the days of apartheid if a black person was walking down the street and they were met by a white person coming from the opposite direction on the sidewalk, they were to step out into the street and allow the white person to walk on the sidewalk. Only this time when the white person approached that young black boy only five years old, he looked down to him and said, "Well, how are you young man? I hope you are having a good day." As he was speaking, the white man stepped out into the street and allowed the little boy and his mother to walk down the sidewalk. As he walked past the man the little boy looked to his mother and said, "Mama, who is that?" She said, "That is the Bishop of the church." The little boy said, "I want to be a Bishop, too." And it was in the heart of that five year old little boy that the desire to be a Bishop was born and he became Bishop Desmond Tutu. You never know! You just never know what one day might bring. You never know what one person might become and we never know who that one person might be. It could be the person that we minister to or the person that we do not minister to.

You have heard the story of the fellow in the General Store of Plains, Georgia, who had his camera around his neck and was bragging. He said, "I have traveled this distance and I have a picture. I have a photograph which I made just a little while ago of the very church that the former President Jimmy Carter worships in today. I have a photograph of it and I want to take it back and show people and tell them I have been right there in the very Baptist Church in Plains, Georgia, where President Carter worships." The fellow at the store scratched his head and said, "Well, Let me ask you something. Was there a fellow down there mowing the grass?" "Yeah! There was an old man down there mowing the grass. I asked him to stop long enough for me to make the picture. He courteously did so and stood over to the side and let me make all the pictures I wanted. As I left he went back to mowing." The owner of the general store said, "Well, it is a shame you did not get a picture of that old man mowing the grass because then you would have not only have a picture of the church in which President Jimmy Carter worships, you would have a picture of President Jimmy Carter." You never know!

We never know. Did Abraham know? Did he get up that morning and say I am going to talk to God today? Probably not! Did Mary get up that morning and in despair, dejection and depression say, "Well, I think I will see the living Jesus today." No, it was a surprise. Life is full of these marvelous, wonderful, serendipitous surprises of God. You notice that both groups in the Parable were surprised. The group was surprised when they learned that by doing their simple acts of generosity, of kindness, of loving, and of compassion they were actually ministering to Jesus. They were totally surprised. They weren't doing this out of any sense of reward or trying to earn their salvation or any sense of assuring their salvation. They were just doing it in such a beautiful way because they were loving, generous and kind. That very nature! On the other hand the other group was also surprised. Wait a minute! When did we see you, Lord, naked or hungry or in prison or in need? If we had known it was you, we would have done something for you. Of course they would? They had been calculating, scheming and playing the angles and system all of their lives. You get ahead by playing the system and using the angles. If it benefits me I will do it. Jesus said no and it doesn't work that way. It doesn't work that way. That is His standard of judgment. We may not like it, but it is His standard of judgment. That is what he is going to do.

It is sorta like the individual who went through the National Art Gallery and stood there, rubbed his chin and said, "I don't like these pictures." And the attendant said, "Sir, the photographs are not on trial." God is not on trial. Neither is his standard of judgment on trial. We are!! Some of us are going to win at life and some of us are not going to win at life. Some of us are going to pass the test and some of us are going to fail the test and it is made up each and every day of those small little decisions in which we contribute. Are we a part of the answer or are we a part of the problem?

It is sorta amazing here that this is the only parable where he tells what he looks like. You never know. We know now. We know what Jesus looks like. Some things we may not know and some things we may never know, but according to this parable we know exactly what Jesus looks like. Jesus looks like human need and in seeing human need we see Jesus Christ. In serving human need we actually serve Jesus Christ and in not serving.... well, you know that story.

C. S. Lewis says when the author comes on the stage the play is over. There will come a day when the author will come on the stage the play will be over. Jesus takes his place as the master and ruler of the universe and his standard of judgment will be levied. How have we responded to human need and in essence how have we responded to Him? Have we responded out of the nature and character of our lives that-is within because He placed it there? His name is Pietro Bandinelli. He was found by Leonardo da Vinci when da Vinci went to paint the Last Supper. It took da Vinci years to paint the Last Supper. It was a very long and trying procedure. The biggest task was finding individuals to accurately display by their faces the different apostles and Jesus in particular. He found Jesus fairly quickly.

His name was Pietro Bandinelli, a young man whose face was alive and full of life and vibrancy. He chose that young man and painted his face as the face of Jesus. He found the other apostles, but the one that he had the most difficulty finding was Judas. How do you find the face that portrays that kind of misguided zeal, if you will, bigotry on one hand, betrayal on the other? How do find a face that portrays that? He searched for a long time and finally traveled the back alleys of the cities and there he found the man. It was a man who was a beggar, a thief, a murderer, a man who had thrown away everything decent he had ever known in all of his life. He hired him to come and be painted. The man came and sat in da Vinci's study for several sittings and then when he went to pay him he asked for his name and the man said, "Why Master, don't you remember me. I am Pietro Bandinelli, the man who served as the face of Jesus. You never know! Sometimes you never know. But one thing we do know according to this word, in seeing our brother and sister in need and in responding to that need we respond to Christ. If you want to see Jesus, look around you. He is everywhere. That you know!!

The Least of These
Matthew 5:31-46

There was an expectant air in the courtroom as the officer of the court entered and said, "Hear ye! Hear ye! Please rise. The Honorable..." With that the defendant rose to his feet. When he saw the judge he literally could not believe his eyes. He rubbed his eyes trying to adjust them is if something were wrong. Immediately his mind flashed to the previous night. It was their twenty-seventh wedding anniversary. They were observing it in the restaurant where they had observed each anniversary. It was a ritual. They were at their favorite table by the window. They loved that table. Not only was it the table of twenty-seven years ago, but the energy and vitality of New York City at night invigorated them. As he was cutting into his filet mignon, he looked up and there in the window was a face, a haunting face, a striking face, the face of a beggar. His hair was long and black. His beard long and dirty. He had scars all over his forehead. It was a disturbing face. Those eyes pierced through his soul. He was so disturbed at the face that he summoned the waiter, "Would you please ask this man to leave? How do you expect me to enjoy my meal with that beggar in the window?" The waiter asked the beggar to leave. He and his wife continued their conversation. "Honey, you seem upset. Is it your court appearance tomorrow?" "No, not really. I'm really not worried about that. Once they understand who I am in this community, how much money I give to charity, how many goodwill programs I support, and all that I have done for this city and my neighborhood. I don't think there will be a problem. My defense is who I am and what I've done. They will see that the charges are small and insignificant."

The judge sits at the bench. By that time the defendant's stomach is in a knot. His palms are sweating, and perspiration has popped out all over his forehead. He thinks he is going to be sick to his stomach. Something has happened that he would never have believed in a hundred, a thousand, or a million years. The judge, his judge, is the beggar at the restaurant window from the night before. Do you feel, do you hear the irony in that?

Do you feel the surprise? Jesus told His disciples, "Boys, don't be surprised when this happens. You will remember I told you. You'll remember I told you how it was going to be. According to Matthew, this is the sermon that Jesus preached to His disciples. This was His concluding public discourse. Now if you were leaving a group of people and you wanted to leave them with one thought, what would you say? Jesus said "Don't be surprised boys because this parable is a summation of all I've ever tried to teach you. It's the heart of the Old Testament. It is Old Testament and Christian justice, law and grace all rolled into one single story, so don't be surprised boys when it happens."

Do you see the scene? Jesus is on the throne. He has already come back and He is now taking His place as Lord and Ruler, King of the universe. All the nations are gathered before him. No one is absent. No one is late. We're all there. I'm there. You're there. Everyone is there and Jesus begins the separation. Only Jesus can do the separating. Jesus is the only one who is qualified to separate the sheep from the goats, the loving from the unloving, those on the right from those on the left. Only Jesus can do that. The criteria is not in question. This script has been written. This has been in God's mind from the very foundation of the world.

A visitor once went into the National Art Gallery and made the flippant remark, "I don't like these pictures." The attendant said, "Sir, the pictures are not on trial." Jesus' standard of judgment is not on trial. That has been determined before the foundation of the world. We are on trial, and we stand before a judge with the face of the beggar in the restaurant window.

Then we feel the surprise. The scene is full of surprises. Everyone is surprised in one way or another. We're surprised that the separation is according to service, not according to what one owned, spent, accumulated or attained, but is according to service - simple acts of kindness and love. Note the simplicity of the service. Simple acts of visiting someone in prison, visiting the sick, clothing the naked, feeding the hungry. Simple acts of everyday Christian kindness and love that all of us can do. There is a certain freedom here. There's a certain spontaneity here. There's a certain un-calculated-ness here, and both groups are surprised. The loving are surprised. "Lord, we didn't know we were ministering to you. We saw someone who needed something and we gave it to him or her. That's what we were doing, just what came naturally. Just doing what we should do, not for reward, just doing it." The unloving are just as surprised. "Lord, if we had known it was you. If we had only known. Why didn't you put VIP on your forehead or something? We thought he was just a beggar in a restaurant window, just someone in the nursing home wasting away that no one came to see, just a hungry person needing something to eat or, something to wear. "Lord, we did not know it was You. If we had only known it was you…SURPRISE! SURPRISE!

The separation is not only according to service, but it is a simplistic service at that. Another surprise is the subject of the service and that is Jesus Himself. Abraham and Sarah were in a dusty tent on a hot dry day when three strangers came to their doorway. Strangers - they entertained angels of God. Two disciples were walking down a road to Emmaus in despair and gloom when a stranger joins them and after fellowship and table communion they discover He is the risen Christ. Mary is on her way to the tomb when she meets a stranger and finds the living Jesus. You never know. We never know. Hot dry days, dusty tents, moments of gloom and despair on the road to we know not what. And we experience Jesus.

Why did come see and some not see? Why were some able to perceive and some only saw? What made the difference? What was the difference between the loving and the unloving, the sheep and the goat, the ones on the right and the ones on the left? I don't know. It could possibly be something like this. Ralph Sockman used to tell that we really have three organs of vision. One organ of vision are those marvelous organs that are within our eye sockets, our eyes, which enable us to see the surface and appearance of things. We're able to look at it and tell the color, the texture, the shape, and form. We see the externals. These are the eyes of the body.

He goes on to talk about another set of eyes through which we see and these are the eyes of the mind. Once we see something we investigate it with the eyes of the mind. We see its shape, its color, its texture, and then we began to make associations. We began to relate that to other things we have seen. The mind begins to look for relationships to others. It is the eyes of the mind, not just the eyes of the body that seeks to connect and associate.

But then Sockman talks about another set of eyes; the eyes of the heart. These are eyes that go to a deeper level and began to ask questions about meaning and significance and purpose. They begin to question the origin of things, the source of things and what does the existence of those things signify. What is their meaning and what is their relationship to me?

Gettis McGregory tells a little story of his own experience and I think it might shed some light. He said that when he was only five years old something happened that influenced his life forever. He was in another room and over heard two couples talking, his mother and father and aunt and uncle. His aunt and uncle told his mother and father, "You know we are so happy that you decided to go ahead and have little Gettis. He is such a source of joy to us." Partially at five, more so later on, he heard those words to say this, "You know I could not have been. At one time at least it was a decision of whether or not I would even be here. But now that I'm here. What does it mean?" And from that he learned that all of life is gift. All of life is grace.

The very reason, the very fact that we are here is gift and grace out of God's benevolence. Love's gift to us. We are here because God wanted us to be here. We are here because God loves us, and because God is in all, and all are in God.

When we see a beggar on the street with his piercing eyes and scarred forehead peering at us as we eat our filet, it is for a purpose. He is there because God loves him and we are there to meet his needs. The very fact that we are here is grace. It's gift. All of life is gift. We are here because God wanted us here. God is in all. And all is in God. I personally can say that when I look back upon the past five years and when I look back upon the last twenty-five years, "It's all grace. It's all gift." To think that God would bless me with the family that I have, the loving church family that I am privileged to serve and the Lord that I am grateful to know and I can say it's gift. It's all gift. It's all grace. God is in all and all are in God.

A Good Neighbor
Luke 10:25-37

A man came to Jesus with a question. He came to Jesus with a question and Jesus responded with a question. The man then came with another question and Jesus again responded with a question. It is a good way to teach, they say.

The first question was a good question. How do I inherit eternal life? Or you might phrase it in a manner of, what is the purpose of my living or how can I have a fuller and richer life? It was a good question and Jesus responded with a question. "Well, have you heard of the Bible? What do you think about that?" And the man said, "Yeah, that is pretty good. 'You should love the Lord God with all your heart, mind and soul and your neighbor as yourself.'" Jesus said. That ain't bad. But then the man took a little twist to the conversation. Luke says he was trying to justify himself and he said, "Who is my neighbor?"

Jesus told a parable and responded with another question. It is a method of teaching, I think, to respond to a question with a question. It was quite well known among the Jewish Rabbis that they would respond to a question with a question. John Claypool says he once asked a Jewish Rabbi, "Why when you are asked a question, do you respond with a question?" The Jewish Rabbi said, "Why not?" It is a good method of teaching.

Jesus was not just being flippant here. Jesus was trying to probe into the man's mindset. He wanted to know what was going on with him in order to be able to answer the man appropriately. Jesus wanted to know the basis of his question. Where were the dynamics that caused such a question? Jesus was a spiritual doctor that did not write the same prescription to every patient that walked in the door. He was not like what they called the old country doctor who would first give you a shot and then ask you what was wrong with you. He wanted to find out what was going on. Where are you? What are the needs in your life that would cause you to ask such a question?

The man then went on to the next question in order to justify himself, Luke says. But perhaps even more so to see who really was his neighbor. He was asking a question to find out what is the least I can get by with. I know I have to obey the law. I know I have to love my neighbor. But what is the least I have to do to obey the law and love my neighbor if I can define who my neighbor is. It is sorta like income tax. We all want to, and know, that we need to obey the law and pay our income tax but no one wants to pay a penny more than we are required to pay. It was with that attitude that the expert in the law asked the question, "Who is my neighbor?" Then Jesus told one of the most famous parables of all - the parable of the Good Samaritan. It seems that a man was going, as Jesus said in the tenth chapter, from Jerusalem to Jericho. On a descending road of about thirty six hundred feet, desert on both sides, very winding and frequently inhabited by thieves and robbers, so much so, it was called the bloody way. A man foolishly was traveling by himself when he was beset by robbers; beaten, robbed and left on the side of the road to die. Then a religious official came by, a priest, a man of high standing in society passed by. Then another man also a religious official came by. Then the Samaritan came by.

We remember the Samaritans. They were looked on as religious and social outcasts. The Jews called them half-breeds. They really were a type of people who were on the bottom level of the ladder. They were looked down upon, criticized, and ostracized by everyone. Then the Samaritan comes and no one would have been surprised if Jesus had said the Samaritan also went over there and looked at the man, kicked him a time or two and looked to see if there was any money left. But then the surprise comes.

As so often Jesus did in the parables, the element of surprise catches us off guard. He says that this Samaritan, this despised outcast was the one who made his resources available to the man in need. It is hard to imagine why this man stopped and helped the man. He dressed his wounds, carried him to the inn, put him in the inn, took care of him and then took care of his future needs. And then Jesus posed the question to the expert in the law and said, "Now which one of the three was a neighbor?"

You can just imagine that expert in the law through gritted teeth and reluctantly said, "The man who had mercy." Then Jesus said that is what you ought to do if you want this full and meaningful life you talk about. Why did the Samaritan stop? Why did the other two go by? I don't know. It is interesting to try to look into the story to place ourselves in it and try to guess why one stopped and two did not.

Perhaps the two did not because they were afraid. Maybe it was a trap. Maybe they were afraid of being assaulted themselves. Maybe they were afraid of the unknown. They did not know what would happen so they did not venture over. Perhaps the Samaritan possessed a certain amount of courage. We do know that fear cast out love as with the two who did not stop but it is also true that love cast out fear as with the one who did. Perhaps the Samaritan was able to overcome his own natural fear of the situation and acted in a loving way instead. He was not afraid to take a risk. And many times to share the love of Christ it takes exactly that. The willingness to overcome our own reluctance, even our own fears, and to act in a loving way, even in a risky way, if we are to act as He would have us to. Or perhaps maybe the other two did not have time. They were busy with crowded schedules and on the way to perform the religious services at the Temple or Synagogue. They just really did not have time. Their calendar just simply did not permit it. Then the Samaritan came. Who knows? Maybe he drug out his day timer, palm pilot, whatever and said, "You know, I really don't have anything pressing right now. Why don't I just try to help this individual?"

Years ago they did an experiment at Princeton University where they divided a class of fifteen in three groups of five each. The professor said to the first group, "You have fifteen minutes to get to a certain point on the other side of the campus. He told the second group, "You have forty-five minutes to get to the same point on the other side of the campus. To the third group he said, "You need to get there by five o'clock." Unbeknownst to them the professor had appointed certain members of the drama classes at Princeton to pose as people in need. One was having seizures and was very, very ill. Another was crying and weeping uncontrollably, others were positioned with dire needs. Guess how many stopped. In the first group that had only fifteen minutes to get over there, not a single one. The second group did a little bit better. They had forty-five minutes and two out of the five stopped. The group that had all afternoon who did not have a crowded schedule all five stopped to help the people who were in need. You see, I think it is true that pressure is a moral category. Busyness is a spiritual issue. Crowded schedules really have to do with the basis of what we call being a Christian. We wonder how many times we let people go by when, if we were not so crowded and in such a hurry, we could have stopped and helped them in the name of Christ.

It happened to me this past week. I was in a hurry walking through the church parking lot when I happened to notice a woman sitting on the ledge there right beside our front door. I spoke to her, and she simply responded, "Pray for me." I went on with my busy schedule. I thought later why didn't I stop and asks what would she like for me to pray. It would have only taken a moment. I have prayed for her many times since. But if I had stopped, I would know what to pray for. Hurry is not of the devil; many times hurry is the devil. We wonder how much of the best do we sacrifice on the altar of the good simply because we are in a hurry. Our busy schedules! Our crowded lives!

I think the Samaritan took time. He simply took time whether he had it or not; he took it. And that is what matters. He took time. We have the opportunity this coming Saturday to take time and some of you still may want to sign up. There is still time for you to join us and be in ministry for a half a day or an entire day. What a wonderful opportunity we have to take time to minister to our city. Many of you do it each and every week. What an opportunity we have for all of us to do it at one time this coming week. Maybe the Samaritan simply took the time or maybe the other two who passed by had this judgmental attitude toward the man who had befallen ill.

He was traveling alone on one of the most dangerous roads anywhere. Perhaps they said he was just a fool. He made his bed. Let him sleep in it. Only a fool would travel alone. And to an extent maybe they were right. The Good Samaritan came by and he did not say this man is a fool or this man may not appreciate it or this man may not deserve it. It did not matter. This man needed it. And out of his own compassion he gave to the need.

I have trouble finding in scripture where Jesus said, "I am to occupy a judgment seat." I have looked long and hard but I cannot find a place where Jesus says I am to occupy some kind of seat of judgment on other people. I find several times where Jesus says I am to occupy a stool and take a towel and basin and wash the feet of others and serve the needs of others.

It was Henry Ward Beecher who said, "This world has to be cleaned up by somebody. You are not a child of God if you are ashamed to scrub and scour." Sometimes serving in the name of Jesus means getting a little dirty! Sometimes it means going out of our way to take the towel and basin and wash the feet of dirty humanity. Out of their need the Samaritan gave or maybe he just simply had what they needed. Had you ever thought of that?

We might be able to say you know the other two realized they did not have what they needed to attend to the man so they rushed on and were going to come back. I know that is a stretch, but let's give them the benefit of the doubt. Just maybe that was the case. They were going to come back and see to the needs of the man. I doubt it, but maybe so. And maybe the Samaritan realized he had what they needed. The Bible does say that he had oil, wine, money, a donkey and a willing spirit. All of things the man needed desperately.

You know that is all that God ask of us. He asks us to give out of what we have. He is not asking you to do a single thing that you cannot do. He is not asking you to do a single thing that you do not have the resources to do. He is not asking you to do a single thing that He will not equip you to do. It is all that we can do to simply do what we can. But that is what he expects us to do. To do is to do what we can.

This coming Saturday I am going to be helping to take care of the preschoolers of those who are going out in the community. I love kids. Everybody qualifies there. Anybody can come down here and help me take care of children. There is something everybody can do. If you want to visit the elderly, you can. If you want to visit new community members, you can. If you want to take plants to people, you can. You can help minister to those who have been abused, or homeless, or to children in the Children's Home. You can work on a Habitat House. There is something everybody can do. There is no struggle. You do not have to have a PhD to be a loving neighbor. All you have to do is be there and be willing.

We struggle on this day, July 4th, on how to be neighbor to the world. How we would love for our world to know *shalom*, true peace. Even as our nation is still engaged in war and our loved ones are losing their lives and people on the other side are losing their lives; we struggle with this entire issue as to what it is to be neighbors to the world. Six percent of the world's population - that is us - use up thirty- five percent of the world's energy.

We struggle with the issue of what it means to be neighbor. I wish that we, as a nation, could solve the ills of the world and I wish that I, as an individual, could solve the ills of the world in Chattanooga. But we, as a nation, cannot we, as a church, cannot I, as an individual, cannot But I can do what I can do I can do with what I can, with what I am, where I am. That is all anyone can do. Maybe the man stopped because he had what the man needed. There are people out there every day who need what you can give. We have already talked about how Samaritans were looked down upon by many peoples. They were really treated as outcasts. Many of them took that status in life and became depressed and felt sorry for themselves and gave up. It was said that the Samaritans were distressed people because they were seen as the outcast of the world. It said there was also a group of Samaritans who not only gave lip but gave in to anger and responded as revolutionaries. Sometimes they were even violent. But yet there were even a third group of Samaritans, maybe this man belonged to that group, who was able to take their hurt and their pain, their mistreatment and misfortune and turn them into gifts to give to someone else. They were able to serve others through their own pain and their own difficulty. They were able to say, "I have been there, too. I know how you hurt. Let me help you in your pain."

My uncle Bill, was a marvelous individual. When he was in school he was a brilliant student. I am not talking smart; I am talking brilliant. He had a brilliant mind. Uncle Bill's life did not work out for him the way that he had wished. He had some misfortune. He had some problems and then he found refuge in the bottle. For many years he unsuccessfully fought the battle of the bottle. But then one day he began to win. He joined AA and out of his pain and out of his own problems he became one of the most outstanding speakers for AA anywhere. He would speak many times every week because he was able to say, "Out of my own pain, out of my own problems, I know where you hurt." We all can do that. We all can serve others out of the pain that we feel. We all can extend the love to them that God has extended to us when we hurt as we!

It was Henry Nouwen who quoted the great Jewish tale. He tells of Joshua Ben Levi who meets the prophet Elijah and says, "Where is the Messiah? Is the Messiah here?" Elijah said, "Why don't you ask him?" "Go ask Him? Where is He?" He said "The Messiah is sitting at the gates of the city." "How will I know him?" he asked. "You will find Him," he responded, "sitting among the poor covered with wounds." "How will I know the Messiah among the others who are wounded?" He said, "It is simple. All the others unbind all their wounds at the same time and then bind up all their wounds afterward, the Messiah is different. The Messiah unbinds the wounds one at a time and then rebinds it with this attitude: "Perhaps I will be needed so I unbind only one at a time so I can respond as quickly as possible." You see, we are all wounded healers. Because there is no other kind.

How to Get to Heaven
Luke 10:25-37

A man confined to a wheelchair for the rest of his life volunteers his time to serve soup in the soup kitchen. A Nicaraguan woman gives to an American television reporter her very last bowl of beans. A man infected with the HIV virus moves out of his home and moves into the home of another man who is dying of AIDS and takes care of that man until he dies. Shocking! Disturbing!

It sometimes bothers us that we see examples such as these which remind us that there are those who seem to be weaker than we are, but yet they teach us what it means to care and to love, and, yes, they might even love us. It's disturbing! It's discomforting. It's shocking!

When the original audience heard Jesus' words about the good Samaritan they were shocked, disturbed and did not feel very comfortable. We've heard the story so many times that the good Samaritan is a part of our language and many times we approach a passage of Scripture like this one today and think we already know what it means and indeed we may.

This story has probably built more clinics and homes and hospitals than any other single factor in the history of mankind. A simple story. But it becomes so familiar that we think we already know what it means. Let's look at it today from a biblical point of view. For you see, biblical preaching, preaching from the Bible, means that we let the Bible interpret the Bible. Biblical preaching is just more than taking a passage out of its context and saying what we want to about It. Jesus used this parable to explain what it meant to love God and to love our neighbor as ourselves. Jesus preached a sermon. So let us hear Jesus' sermon. I'll be the first to tell you that I do not know what it means.

There are several different ways of looking at it. We might have an angle upon it like a beautiful diamond held up to the light. We might see different interpretations that fit into the arena of what this marvelous story means. Perhaps this story is saying something about those who seem to have all the answers.

Luke tells us in Verse 25 that an expert in the Law, not an attorney as we know them today, but a religious expert in the Law came to Jesus and said, "How can I get to Heaven?" Jesus said, "Well, what does the Law say?" "Love the Lord thy God with all thy heart, soul, mind and spirit, and love thy neighbor as thyself." Jesus said, "You've done well. You have answered correctly. Now do this and you will live."

Then the Bible says the man seeking to justify himself asked, "Who is my neighbor?" Here was a person who had all the answers. He was an expert In the Law. I mean he averaged a 4.0 but failed to get an education. He had all the answers, but missed the point. He was an expert in the Law, but had no wisdom. And Jesus asked him to probe his mind because Jesus knew this man already knew the answers to the questions that he asked.

He had no desire whatsoever to put into practice the answers. He was only trying to test Jesus. He was looking for loop holes. He was looking for the easy way. "How can I exclude someone?" "Tell me whom I am supposed to love where I can love them and not love those people that I'm not supposed to love." "What is the easy way to get to Heaven?"

Sometimes we believe that's the way we will take. We think that if we use our mouth or put something into our mouth that everything will be all right. If we take this pill or if we eat this food or if we go on this diet or if we fill the air with a barrage of words that everything will be okay. Food, a pill, a drug. That's the easy way.

I remember several years ago, Lou Ferrigno, the Incredible Hulk, and Mr. Muscles was on the *Merv Griffin Show*. He took off his shirt and WHAT MUSCLES! Merv said, "What in the world do you eat to get all of those muscles?" He said, I just eat vegetables and fruits and meats, but I exercise a lot." "No! What do you eat? Tell me what is magic that I can put in my mouth!" The easy way. "Which book can I read? What seminary can I go to? What course can I take? What creed can I believe? What can I adhere to that will give me all of the answers?"

The expert in the Law was trying to reduce faith to a debate, as if faith were a debate, and it consisted of who's right and who's wrong. It consisted of those who would formulate systems of belief so correct that they could make all the rules, sit in on judgment of others and from a vantage point say, "I am right and you are wrong. Now you must do what I say.

So often we get paralysis from analysis. We sit around debating and debating and the world goes to Hell in a hand basket. The essence of real faith is more than just something we do with our mouth. It is more than just something we do with our mind. It is something that we have in our heart. It is a personal relationship to the living Lord Jesus Christ. That is the essence of our faith and the source of the love that we have for God and the source of the love that we have for ourselves and that is the source of the love that we have for each other. So maybe this episode in scripture has something to do with those who seem to have all the answers.

Or maybe it has something to do with those that we are supposed to love. Here was a man along the side of the road, beaten and robbed, left half-dead; Levite comes by, priest comes by, no one stops. A Samaritan comes by and stops. Why? The man was in need. He needed something and without some help he would surely die. We sometimes back off and say, 'Well, do they deserve it?" "Will they appreciate it?" Jesus said, "You must ask the question, 'Do they need it?'" This Samaritan took care of a Jew, and the Samaritans hated the Jews and the Jews hated the Samaritans, but it didn't matter because here was a man in need. It wasn't a moral question. It wasn't a religious question. It was a question of help and he helped.

This parable attacks and challenges every form of bigotry, every form of prejudice, every form of stereotyping and every form of any way that we seek to categorize and exclude. The Samaritan helped a Jew even though the Jews and the Samaritans were enemies. Jesus said, "If you love only those who love you what reward have you? Even the heathen do that." Jesus said, "You love, yes, you love, even those that you would consider to be your enemy. You love those whom you don't understand. You love those that you fear. You love those that don't understand you. You love those and do good to those who would even seek to do harm to you." That's the love that Jesus is talking about. Who are those we are to love? We are to love the needy, and we are to love our enemies.

Leslie Weatherhead tells the story of a young Armenian woman whose home was broken into by Turkish soldiers. They took her mother, her father and her brothers out into the front yard and shot them. They took her and her sisters and used them in a disgraceful way, and then threw them into a Turkish prison. She escaped and went back to the Armenians and there she was taught to be a nurse.

One night in an Armenian hospital as she was taking care of the wounded soldiers she noticed a prisoner of war. As she looked in the bed, she recognized the face. It was the leader of the group that had killed her family and the very one that had abused her. All she had to do was just leave him alone and let him die. Do nothing but she could not. She nursed him back to health.

The Armenian doctor told the Turkish soldier, "Without this nurse you would have died." And the Turkish soldier said, "I know, we've met before." And he asked the young Armenian nurse, "Why did you do it? After all have done to you, why didn't you just let me die?" She said, "I could not. For you see, the one I follow said, 'Love your enemies.' That is my faith and I could do no other." And he said to her, "I want to know about that kind of faith." Maybe Jesus is talking about those that we are to love.

Or maybe Jesus was talking about how we are to love them. We are not only to love without boundaries, we are to love without any expectation of recompense. We are to love in a frivolous, spontaneous and extravagant kind of way.

Look again, here was a man who delayed his own journey and took a personal risk to himself at great danger. Here was a man who expended a great deal of energy. Here was a man "who spent two days" wages with a promise of much more to expend. Here is a man who followed up on the person that he helped, and the person that he helped would consider him to be a social outcast, a religious heretic and a person with a bad reputation. That is not a profile easily duplicated. It tells how we are to love. We are to love with no boundaries, with no expectation of recompense. We are to simply love because it is God's nature to love and God's nature is within us. When Jesus told the expert in the Law, "Now, you go, and do likewise.' Do you think he did? I doubt it, because he had missed the point.

First Corinthians says, "If I speak with the tongues of men and angels (James Glass calls these the enthusiasts) but have not love, I am only a resounding gong or a clanging cymbal. If I have the gift of all prophecy and all knowledge (egg heads) fathom all mysteries and have not love, it I have the faith to remove mountains (prayers) and if I give my body to be burned and give all that I have to feed the poor (chicken fryers) and have not love I am nothing." What is he saying? I think he is saying that we can do all these things and not love, we can have great knowledge, we can be very enthusiastic, we can do great works and we can even be spiritual to a point, and not love. But if we love, we will do all those things and more, and I think that is what he is saying.

If at the very heart and essence and basis of our faith is the love of Jesus Christ then we cannot help but do all of those things. We cannot help but stop and take pity. We cannot help but do as Jesus commanded the expert. For you see, when we love, we will do. It's that simple. It's at the heart. It's the essence of our faith.

Maybe Jesus is talking about those who seem to have all the answers. Maybe He is talking about those that we are to love and maybe He's talking about how we are to love them without boundary and without expectation recompense because it is God's nature in us causing us to do so. But maybe there is another light, maybe there is another angle upon this old story that we have not yet considered. Stay with me here! Maybe this story is about those from whom we are to accept love. Think about that.

You see, it sometimes gets difficult that we are to accept love from those who seem to be weaker than we are and those that sometimes we are even tempted to look down upon. Sometimes we think that we are superior to them in some ways; morally, mentally, physically, and spiritually and that we are not to accept love from them. The good Samaritan is the man in the wheelchair that serves soup at the soup kitchen? The good Samaritan is the Nicaraguan woman who gives up her last bowl of beans. The good Samaritan is the HIV infected man who helps another man die. We don't want to hear that. Oh, how discomforting it is because we want to be in control, we want to be in charge. We want to be the one that does the giving. We want to be the one who gives and ministers and controls and is in a position of superiority. We do not want to become open. We do not want to become vulnerable. We do not want people to know that we are weak, and that we might have to accept what they have to give and accept the love. We do not want to accept that there are good Samaritans everywhere who can and will help us and love us and in our weakness we are touched by their love.

Christine Smith, an excellent preacher, tells the story of a friend of hers by the name of Kay. Kay was walking down a street in New York City when she noticed an elderly lady rummaging through the garbage. Kay, being a Christian, walked up to her and said, "May I give you my lunch?" The woman responded, "No, thank you I have already eaten," and went back to rummaging in the trash cen. Kay walked on a step or two and then turned around to face the woman again and the woman rummaging around in the trash can looked up and just froze a moment and then asked, "Do you need me to eat your lunch?" Kay answered, "Yes." Sometimes it is very discomforting to accept love.

Who are you in this parable? The priest? The Levite, too busy with religion to stop and help someone? Are you the man on the side of the road, life has beaten out of you and you don't care who they are, you just need someone to help you, to touch your life with a word of mercy and touch your life with grace?

Are you the good Samaritan whom others might see as weak and may even look down on you; but yet your heart overflows with love? Or are you the expert today who has trouble admitting that he or she is in as much need of grace and mercy as the man on the road? Can you admit your weakness today? Can you admit your sinfulness today? Can you admit your helplessness today and let God do for you what only He can do? For you see, He was beaten. He was spit upon. He was disgraced. He was humiliated. He was hung naked between Heaven and Hell and despised and rejected by the people He came to save. Will you let Him love you today? Will you let His mercy be yours? Will you let His grace live in your heart? He's waiting to touch your life. Have you ever acknowledged Him as your Lord and Savior? Have you ever repented of your sins and asked Jesus to come into your life, take control of your life and to be your Lord and Savior forever?

You can today.

The Original Prayer
Luke 11:1-13

The Gospel of Luke chronicles the prayer life of Jesus like no other gospel. At least six times in the Gospel of Luke the Scriptures tell us that Jesus went to pray at times that are not mentioned in the other gospels. Luke tells us that Jesus' baptism experience occurred during a time of prayer. The Bible tells us that Jesus' temptation experience occurred during a forty day prayer retreat; that before Jesus chose His disciples, He spent an entire night in prayer; that the transfiguration experience occurred during a time of prayer; that when Peter made his declaration that Jesus was the Messiah was during a time of prayer.

In the Ninth Chapter, Verse 51 of Luke, Jesus had resolutely and absolutely set His face toward Jerusalem and all that would occur there. The disciples came to Him and said the original prayer which is: "Lord, teach us to pray." Why did they come to Jesus and ask Him to teach them to pray? They had been following Jesus a long time, as much as a year or possibly two. I really don't know why they asked Jesus to teach them to pray, but as we look into the first ten chapters of the Gospel of Luke perhaps the Bible will teach us why the disciples uttered the original prayer.

Perhaps the disciples had seen in Jesus a power resource that Jesus had found in prayer. Maybe Jesus' own example of prayer had caused them to ask the question: Lord, teach us to pray. No doubt they had seen Jesus on many occasions tired and totally exhausted by all the demands that were placed upon Him, and then they would see Him retreat, spending time with the Father, returning revitalized and energized. No doubt, many times they had seen Him, drained by all of the pressure and the stress, arise early in the morning before anyone else and spend time with the Father. Perhaps it was the example of Jesus that caused them to say, "Lord, teach us to pray."

Kierkegaard said of his generation, (and it pertains to ours as well), that his generation was dying for lack of passion. Ask yourself, is there anything about which you are really excited? Is there anything in your life today about which you feel a sense of urgency? Is there anything in your life today about which you feel enthusiasm? Do you feel a sense of urgency? Are you praying for it today? Is there anything in your life that you can pray for?

Perhaps the disciples asked Jesus to teach them to pray because they were being pushed as never before. They were called to go out and witness. They were called to go out and heal. They were called to go out and preach and teach. They were called to go into villages with no support, depending totally upon the village to provide food and shelter. They were called to go armed with nothing but the Holy Spirit. Now how can you do that without prayer?

Perhaps the disciples came to Jesus asking, "Lord, teach us to pray," because they were asked to forgive their enemies. And how can you do that without prayer? Or perhaps the disciples asked Jesus to teach them to pray because they had experienced failure. You remember as Jesus, Peter, James and John were on the Mount of Transfiguration in that marvelous transforming experience; down below in the valley, the poor disciples were mired in deep failure and disgust. A man brought to them his son who was ill and asked the disciples to heal the boy and they could not. Before they had healed and now they could not. They were faced with the depth of their own spiritual poverty and their inability and failure to do what God had equipped them to do. They were humbled by their own failure. Is there one of us who has not known that feeling? How do you cope with failure without prayer?

Or perhaps the disciples came to Jesus and asked Him to teach them to pray because they had experienced success. The twelve were sent out in the ninth chapter of Luke two by two. The seventy, in the tenth chapter, were sent out two by two and both times they had experienced great success. They came back so excited. "Lord, you should have seen what we were able to do In Your name!" We all know, don't we? Every one of us knows that success is harder to handle than failure. I hope that none of us are so naive as to think that everything that is successful in our world is blessed by God. Just because something has great numbers to it and just because something is glitzy and flashy does not mean that God is blessing that. Sometimes it is just the opposite.

You will remember that Solomon started out so well as the King of Israel. He did everything so right and then all of a sudden he was doing everything so wrong that he put his country in a terrible predicament. Solomon caused the nation of Israel to split forever. And how did God punish him? God continued to give him everything he wanted. It is sort of like having too much chocolate cake. After a while it is not good. One of the worst things is to always have your way. Success is hard to handle, and I don't know anyone who can handle success properly without prayer.

Or perhaps the disciples came to Jesus with the request to be taught to pray because Jesus had begun to talk about His own death. When Peter made his declaration that Jesus was the Messiah, Jesus then begin to tell them, "And yes, the Messiah must go to Jerusalem and there He will be killed." Simon

Peter said, "No! Wait a minute! Not you, Lord! It won't happen to you, Lord!" Start talking about death and all of a sudden the room will get quiet.

Start talking about death to your children or your grandchildren and the room will get quiet. Start talking about funeral arrangements or pre-arrangements or living wills or wills and all of a sudden the room gets quiet. We don't want to talk about death. Jesus started talking about death and Simon Peter said, "No! No! Let's not talk about that." Some things are just difficult to talk about, and that is why prayer must be learned. That's why the disciples said, "Lord, teach us to pray."

Someone might say that prayer is just the heart's natural desires coming out. No! Not according to the Bible. Prayer is taught; prayer is disciplining; prayer is something that we learn from God and from Jesus and learn from His word. I don't know anyone who is good at prayer. Do you? I know some people who treat prayer glibly, and I know some people who can pray eloquently. Paul said that no one really knows how to pray. But there is a Spirit within us that communicates with God's Spirit. Romans, the Eighth Chapter, tells us that the Spirit intercedes with us and for us. But let us not treat prayer as something glib and something we think we are good at.

A young man gave a devotion in Los Angeles several years ago during the racial tensions. He treated the devotion in a very glib way, and at the end, a black minister came up to him and said, "My friend, don't ever talk about prayer again until you have stood as I have in the face of a locked door and knocked for seventy years with bloody knuckles. Prayer is difficult. And if you don't believe prayer is difficult look at the Garden of Gethsemane experience where Jesus prayed for hours and hours in such a stressful position that even the sweat on His brow became as blood. Jesus began to talk about death and serious things and the only way you can do that is through prayer. Perhaps that is why the disciples said, "Lord, teach us to pray."

Maybe the disciples came to Jesus because things were getting too big for them. You know, too big. This nice little Jewish kingdom for us four and no more. Jesus began to let in sinners, tax collectors, prostitutes, the downcast, and the rift-raft of society. Jesus began ministering to them. Jesus began to minister to little children and children didn't count in their eyes, but they counted in Jesus' eyes. Jesus began to let the women in.

There was even a group of women who went with Jesus everywhere and supported Jesus and the disciples financially. He began to let the women in, he began to let the children in, he began to let the sinners in, and Jesus began to let the Romans in. The Roman Centurions. He even let the Samaritans in! "This thing is just getting too big for us," they said.

Jesus even touched a leper. You can have problems when you are part of something like that and they start letting in people that you don't want to associate with and that you don't want to be seen with. So perhaps that is why the disciples went to Jesus and said, "Lord, teach us to pray."

Dr. Fred Craddock tells of a prayer meeting several years ago during the Iraqi war. A young man led in the opening prayer and in doing so he prayed: "Lord, be with the women and children in Iraq who are going to be killed tomorrow." At the end of the prayer meeting a man came up to him and asked, "Why did you pray like that? Are you for Saddam?" He said, "Of course not, but I wanted to pray for the women and children." The man said, "Well, you prayed for the wrong people."

How can anyone pray for the wrong people? You see this kingdom that Jesus came to start is big and it just keeps getting bigger and bigger. And if it gets too big for us, our only alternative is to come to Jesus and say, "Lord, teach us to pray."

Perhaps there was just a mystery about the Kingdom of God that the disciples did not understand. So, Jesus taught them to pray and He taught them that prayer is not something you understand; prayer is not something you do well, prayer is not something at which you become an expert; prayer is not just something you memorize and repeat eloquently, but prayer is nurturing your personal relationship with Jesus. Prayer is not, "Give me, give me." Prayer is not just listening. Prayer is nourishing a relationship and like any other relationship that you want to go well, you must give it time, attention and energy and you must never take prayer for granted.

Think about the loved ones in your life. What if you never gave them any time? What if you never gave them any attention? What if you took them for granted all of the time and the only time you wanted to spend some time with them was when you wanted something from them? What kind of relationship would you have? It is the same with God. He is our Heavenly Father and prayer is the nurturing of that relationship with Him. No matter how much we grow in knowledge there will always be a mystery.

My wife and I have been married forty-eight years, and we dated several years before. I probably know her as well as I know any other human being, but there are times when she is a total mystery to me, and she is smart enough to keep it that way. Even in the closest and most intimate relationships there is always an element of mystery and so should it be. Prayer is not based upon a complete understanding.

Prayer is based on the nurturing of a relationship with God. So we come to Him and say, "Lord, we don't understand, but we see something in you that is so inviting." "Teach us to pray," and Jesus says to pray for deliverance from your enemies and forgive your enemies. We pray for daily bread and He gives us a job to do. We pray for understanding and He says, "I will give you my presence." We pray and He gives to us the sweet, sweet Holy Spirit. He promises to be with us and never to forsake us. How wonderful that is!

In 1824 the United States was undecided about its next president. In the election neither John Quincy Adams nor Andrew Jackson received a majority vote. The outcome of the election was tossed into the House of Representatives. The States were also equally divided. It finally came down not only to one state, the state of New York, but to ONE delegate. ONE SINGLE DELEGATE! He was asked by Henry Clay to vote for John Quincy Adams, but he replied, "I don't like the man, but I will tell you what I will do. I will pray about it and seek God's will in the matter." That one single delegate from New York went to bed that night and prayed until he found God's answer. Through prayer he helped to elect the next President of the United States and also helped to determine the direction of our country. Oh, what God can do with one person who says, "Lord, teach me to pray?" Will you be that person? I think it is now time to pray.

Faithfully Claiming the Future
Luke 12:13-21

You may have seen the television episode of ER where a relatively young man was brought to the emergency room because he had been exposed to an acid of some kind. They told him that such an exposure to such a compound would literally drain the calcium from his body and that it was fatal. The man who looked healthy as a horse said, "You mean I'm going to die?" And the doctors reluctantly said, "Yes." He asked, "How long do I have? Months? Years?" And the doctor said, "You have twelve hours to live." Twelve hours to live!! What do you think that man thought about?

The Bible tells us that Jesus was teaching when a man came to Him and said, "Teacher, make my brother divide up the inheritance." But Jesus refused to get into that trap. The man already knew what the law said. Jesus refused to give in to the greed that prompted the man's question. Instead Jesus told a parable, and used it as an occasion to teach His disciples and to teach us. He said there was a farmer who had been very successful. He had a bountiful harvest, and said to himself, "What am I going to do with all of this stuff? This is fantastic! I know what I will do. I will build for myself bigger barns and store it all. Then I will take it easy. I will relax, eat, drink and be merry."

The last word from the man's voice as he shared his inner thoughts with God and as Jesus shared His inner thoughts with us was, "merry." I will eat, drink and be merry." And the first word out of the voice of God was "fool. This night your life will be demanded of you." He didn't say, "right now." He said, "This night." Did this man have a few minutes or a few hours to look back upon his life? What did he think about? If you knew that you had twelve hours or less to live, what would you think about? What do you think he thought about? Maybe he thought that he had wasted his life on a puny premise.

There is such a thing as the Mclandress Coefficient. It is a test devised by Hershell McLandress who was a professor of psychiatric measurement at Harvard Divinity School. He came up with a test that measured one's self-absorption. It measures to what extent we are absorbed with ourselves; and has something to do with our conversations and how long we can go without speaking about ourselves - I - me - mine – myself.

It was said that Eleanor Roosevelt had a McLandress Coefficient of two hours. She could go two hours without talking about herself, John F. Kennedy, twenty-nine minutes and Elizabeth Taylor, three minutes. I wonder what kind of McLandress Coefficient this fellow had. "I, my barns, my crops, my future, I will settle down, I will do this, I will do that." His life was literally lived for himself. What a puny premise! What a shaky foundation! Do you think he thought that he had wasted the most precious gift he had, life itself, on such a puny premise?

In 1975, Robert Burrows went to a yard sale in Nashville, Tennessee. He could not believe his eyes when he saw a black and white lithograph for sale for only $5.00. A woman was selling all of her possessions to join a commune. It was 1975, remember. He bought it and when he got home, he found out that it was exactly what he thought it was, an original Picasso. How tragic to sell such a priceless possession for such an unworthy goal. How sad that a man could give away a wonderful possession, life itself, for such a puny premise, and that's what the man did. The Bible says, "Tonight that which has possessed you that which you thought you possessed, will demand your life from it." That is the way the Bible actually reads. Your possessions will demand your life from you. Cessation was just a belated announcement of a death that had already occurred. This man was about to die physically. He had been dead spiritually for years and was just waiting on somebody to throw dirt over him. Maybe he thought, "I have wasted my life, God's most wonderful gift to me, life itself, on such a puny premise."

Or maybe he went beyond that and thought, "You know, I really have missed the joy of life, and the joy of living." Now notice this wasn't a bad man. The Bible doesn't say he was dishonest. The Bible doesn't say that he mistreated anyone. The Bible doesn't say that in any way he was a drain upon society. In fact, he was probably an upstanding person in society and was seen by all as a man of upstanding qualities. They believed in Jesus' day that if you were wealthy it was because God was blessing you, and in an indirect way, please hear me, that is true. Because Romans 12 says that if you have the gift to earn money and use it for God's purposes that is a gift of God. The ability to earn money and use it for God's purposes is, in fact, a gift of God. He didn't understand that, and he did not understand that there was an interconnectedness between his life and the life of those around him. He thought that he was given everything for his benefit and not given through him on the way to others.

All three of my children were not born in a state of the United States. They were born in Kentucky which is a Commonwealth. Commonwealth - have you thought of that idea? There is that interconnectedness to life, there is an inter-relatedness that we have one with another and our possessions are not just ours, and they belong to everybody. There is a commonness to them because you see everything I have ever attained and everything I have ever hoped to be in many ways I owe to other people. The education I received, the very life that I have. The opportunities that I have received I owe in some way to others. Every road I walk upon has been paved by someone else, and to realize the inter-connectedness we have with each other is a marvelous, joyful thing. It is the joy of life. And maybe he thought to himself, "I missed it. I never got life!"

But I think the greatest tragedy in this man's life and sometimes in our lives is that we miss the joy of giving. There is no greater joy in our existence than the joy of being able to give to other people and be able to go to bed at night and think that because God has so blessed me, I was able to give back to God and to His purposes. Because I gave, someone tonight is fed, someone tonight has an opportunity to go to work, and someone tonight is in a warm bed. Someone tonight has a home in which to live, and someone tonight has heard because of my gift and someone today has heard about the blessed love and grace of our Lord and Savior Jesus Christ.

Isn't the greatest joy of life being able to give of our resources, our talents, our time and ourselves to someone else? Is there a greater joy in scripture or in life than to see that our lives are an investment in the lives of others? We are here in our interconnectedness and relatedness not only to have a good life but to see that others have a good life as well. We can invest in the lives of others.

When the Cooperative Program was adopted in 1925, in an association in Missouri there were twenty-two churches, and only three churches said they would be a part of the Cooperative Program. Nineteen churches said, "We will be a part of the Cooperative Program when we have won all of the lost people in our city to Christ." On this day of those twenty-two churches the nineteen churches who refused to join the Cooperative Program are no longer in existence and the three who joined are. It's called "making an investment in the lives of other people." I don't know what the man thought about. Maybe he had just a few minutes or maybe hours, but I got to thinking about that myself. What would I leave behind? Would it matter that I had been here? Would other lives be richer or poorer because Gary Carver walked on the face of this planet?

Karl Valentino was, what was called back in the 1930's, one of the metaphysical clowns of Europe. Sort of like some of the clown figures of our day. He dressed like a clown and acted like a clown but yet he illustrated eternal truth. On a stage in Munich, Germany in 1931, he went to the stage dressed as a clown. All there was upon a darkened stage was a circle of white light. The clown got down on his hands and knees and was searching for something in the lighted circle. A policeman walked by and asked him, "Sir, what are you doing?" He replied, "I'm searching for my house keys. I have lost my house keys and I cannot get into my house without them." With that the policeman began helping the clown look for his keys within the circle of light. Finally, the exasperated policeman said, "Are you sure you lost the keys here?" The clown said, "No, I lost the keys over there (pointing to a dark place on the stage)." The policeman asked him, "If you lost the keys over there why are you looking over here?" And he said, "Because there is no light over there." May we not be guilty of looking for something where it does not exist.

Cost Analysis
Luke 14:25-33

It costs a lot to say "yes" to God.

The old man lumbered across his small apartment after finishing a light meal. On this day his apartment seemed emptier and lonelier than it had ever been. It was a modest apartment. He can tell you to the day how long it has been since his beloved wife Bonnie went on to be with the Lord -- six months, two weeks, four days. It still hurts. The ache is constant. But this day rivaled any day. He feels more alone on this day than perhaps he has ever felt in all of his life, because on this day he said, "Goodbye" to his only child, his daughter.

What would he have done without her these last few months? As he had always done, he knelt beside his bed and prayed, "Oh, God, I need you today. Please fill this emptiness with your presence. When Bonnie and I thought that we could never have a child, we prayed asking you to give us a child and we promised to give that child back to you, I just didn't think you would ask so soon. And now she, too, is gone. Oh, God, fill the emptiness that is within my heart. Give me patience." And with that the old man crawled into bed and stared at the ceiling with eyes that would not find sleep, because on this morning he said, "Goodbye" to his only child and his only grandchild as they left for Kenya and the mission field. It cost a lot to say "yes" to God.

There were huge crowds following Jesus. Jesus was immensely popular. The crowds were wild and enthusiastic as they journeyed toward Jerusalem. Mark and Luke tell us that Jesus turned to the crowds, not to the disciples, and said, "Are you sure you want to follow me? Have you counted the cost?" It is wise to count the cost. If a man is going to build a tower he first has to see if he has the resources to complete the tower or else he will be the subject of ridicule. Or if a king is going to war he will first of all count his resources to see if he has a chance. Without a chance he is needlessly sacrificing his people.

It is important to count the cost. "Do you really want to be my disciple?" Jesus asked the crowds, and then He told them what they must do to be His disciple. He said, "If you will come after me you must hate your mother and father, sisters and brothers and everyone that is dear to you. You must hate even yourself if you are to become my disciple, and you must take up your cross and follow me." That is tough! It cost a lot to say "yes" to God. And Jesus is saying that it is going to cost YOU a lot. Are you sure you want to follow Jesus? Have you counted the cost?

The word "hate" in the original language is a Semitic idiom which means to separate oneself from or to detach oneself from. It is not the hate-filled emotional word that we talk about today which is the opposite of love and the subject of hate-crimes. When Jesus is saying "hate," he means to detach oneself from. As you know, the Bible was not written in English, the Bible was written in Greek, and Jesus did not speak English or Greek. Jesus spoke Aramaic. Jesus was a Semite. And even when Jesus said to hate oneself, He meant that we do not throw ourselves across the threshold of the world and ask everyone to come by and use us as a doormat. Jesus loved Himself and He asked us to love ourselves, and Jesus certainly loved His loved ones. But what does He mean? One translation says, "If you are not willing to take that which is dearest to you, whether it be plans or people, and kiss it goodbye you cannot be my disciple." What is the cost of following Jesus? What does it mean to make Jesus our Lord? What does it mean to be Jesus' disciple? It means that there is no such thing as deep discount discipleship.

When you hear of an outlet mall, you immediately have visions of big stores -- discount prices -- fifty percent off -- bargains galore. Thousands upon thousands of people flood outlet malls with a craving for saving. You don't always find the bargains that you expected to find. There is no such thing as a bargain in discipleship. Discipleship is not like joining a book club. If you join a book club you might get seventeen free books, but when you read the small print it says that in the next three months you have to buy thirty-eight books at triple the price and if you do not fulfill your part of the obligation you have to give up your first born child. It's not exactly a bargain. There ain't no free lunch!

And it is true with Jesus our Lord, but you wouldn't know it by listening to some preachers and by listening to some of the television entertainers on the religious channel. They sell Jesus like He is a used automobile. "Nothing down! Easy terms! No interest! It is all so convenient! Just come on and follow Jesus! Jesus is user friendly! Follow Jesus and you will be healthy, wealthy and wise! Just name it and claim it! Our Jesus aims to please!" What a sham! What a sacrilege!

To our marvelous Savior who died willingly on the cross for us, there is no such thing as a deep discount discipleship. Just the opposite is true. If you are a disciple of Jesus, it will cost you a lot. If you are to be Jesus' disciple, you must make Him number one priority of your life. There is no other substitute. If Jesus is Lord of your life, you are not! Jesus is! And that means when you make Jesus Christ the number one priority in your life everything else is influenced by that single decision.

It was true of Queen Elizabeth. When she was a young child, a princess, she told her uncle, George V, "I'm a princess and because I'm a princess I will do anything I like." And her uncle said, "No, my dear it is because you are a princess that you can never do anything you like." Because we are His we just don't do whatever we like, we do what Jesus likes. Don't you wish it were that clear cut and simple? Don't you wish it were as simple as choosing between Jesus and Satan? How I wish it were that Simple! If it were that simple our decisions would be clear cut, no gray area, everything would be black and white. Jesus said that you must choose between Him and the very dearest that you hold in life, the highest allegiance you have in life. It is not that simple. It does not mean that we cease to love those who are dear to us, it means that we love Jesus more. It means to take up your cross daily.

We sometimes misunderstand what the Bible means by "take up your cross daily." We may think, "Well, I'm sick, and that's the cross that I bear. Or I'm in an unfortunate relationship, and that's the cross that I bear. Or there are some circumstances beyond my control, and that's the cross I bear." No! No! That is not what the Bible means at all when talking about bearing one's cross. Bearing one's cross means the things that we do intentionally and willingly for God, the things we sacrificially give up for Him. It is the sacrifice that we are called upon to make because we are His followers. It means to take up your cross willingly and daily, not an act of emotions, but an act of the will. It simply means that when we call Jesus Christ Lord of our lives, He becomes the top priority of our lives. It redefines every single decision we make in life. Every single decision is made around that singular, total and central commitment to Jesus Christ as our Lord and Savior.

We pay the cost in different ways. Some of us pay the cost of discipleship by the giving of our time, some by the giving of talents, for some it might cost a relationship, for some it might cost money, for some it might cost ego and for some it might cost ambition. Abraham Lincoln assembled his cabinet together and put on the table before them a blank sheet of paper and he said, "I want every one of you to sign this." He asked them to sign a blank sheet of paper and he would fill in the rest. That's what it means to follow Jesus Christ as Lord. We come to Jesus and give to Him everything. We sign our name on a blank sheet of paper and wait for Him to fill in the rest. Our commitment to Jesus as Lord redefines and rearranges all other priorities we might have. For some of us that might mean taking a risk. It might mean getting out of your comfort zone and doing things that God has called you to do as uncomfortable and as unsettling as that might be. You may have heard the story of a traveler passing through. He saw the old farmer sitting on his front porch so he stopped to be sociable and said, "Well, how's your corn doing this year?" The old farmer replied, "Well, I didn't plant any corn. Afraid we might not get enough rain." "How's your cotton doing?" "Well, I didn't plant any cotton either. I'm afraid of the boll weevil." "Well, how's your potatoes coming along?" "Well, you know there are a lot of potato bugs in this part of the country." "Well, what did you plant?" The old farmer said, "I didn't plant anything. I'm playing it safe."

Playing it safe? To follow Jesus Christ as Lord may mean that some of you will have to get outside the comfort zone, quit playing it safe and actually put yourself on the altar and say, "Oh, God, what do YOU want ME to do?" Are you sure you want to be a disciple of Jesus Christ? Have you counted the cost? Are you really sure you want to do this? It cost a lot to say "yes" to God. Some didn't say "yes" to God. Jesus turned to the crowds and asked the question and some thought the price was too high. Some fell away and not everyone accompanied Jesus to Jerusalem.

We are on a journey through this world which is not our own and some are a little bit confused, and I, myself, am sometimes confused about the nature of this journey. Some think the Christian journey is just a big, happy parade through life where everybody is enthused and rejoicing and always having a big time. They are oblivious to cost and conflict and oblivious to Christ's demand upon their life, and when the hard times come and the road is a little rocky, they fall aside. There are others who think the Christian journey is a march and everybody is marching as if going into battle. Everybody is against everybody, and they have a point to prove. They have to prove they are right. It's the good guys against the bad guys. It's the haves against the have nots, it's the liberals against the conservatives, it's the moderates against the fundamentalists, it's the males against the females. For any of them, life is just an angry march. Did Jesus see the Christian life as a parade or as a march proving a point?

For Jesus the march to Jerusalem was not a parade, it was not a march, the journey was a funeral procession. Jesus was going willingly, lovingly and intentionally to Jerusalem to die for you and for me, and that is why the relationship with Jesus Christ is a personal journey. It cost a lot to say "yes" to God. Are you sure you want to do this? Have you counted the cost? It cost a lot to say "yes" to God, but it cost even more to say "no."

Amazing (and Offensive) GRACE!
Luke 15:1-3, 11b-32

We stand on holy ground today. We have just heard the greatest short story ever told. It is a story about God, and this story, other than Jesus Christ Himself, tells us more about God than any other piece of literature in the world. My task today is to let you hear the story, set the context of the story and remove any hindrances that would keep you from hearing the story. The Bible says that people were coming to Jesus and He was having table fellowship with them. They were considered to be sinners. They were people that had been kicked out of the synagogue. They had so many problems and had done so many wrong things they were called sinners by the religious establishment.

Then there were the tax collectors, people who were seen as traitors. They were for Rome and against the Israelite people. The religious establishment, the Pharisees and teachers of the Law, could not believe that Jesus was actually having anything to do with this riff-raff of society. Tax collectors were thought to be immoral and unclean people. Jesus was not only associating with them, He was eating with them! The Pharisees and teachers of the Law felt you had to keep people separated. You separated the good from the bad. You separated the white from the black. You separated the moral from the immoral. You put one group of people in one place and another group of people in another place, and the two shall never meet. If they mingle how in the world can you teach young folks morals? You've got to keep them separated. And there are those in our day who believe such. It is okay to go there and have a Vacation Bible School, but don't bring them here.

This parable is told to us and this parable is told about us. Do not hear this parable as only presenting a dark backdrop. This parable is a diamond, and it is an invitation to party. A party is going on and you're invited. There are at least four groups of people and Carl Olson describes their attitudes about this party. There were those who didn't even know there was as party, there were those who knew there was a party but didn't think they were invited, there were others who knew there was a party, they knew they were invited but they didn't believe they deserved to attend the party, and the fourth group of people knew there was a party, they knew they were invited, they came and enjoyed the party to the limits. They enjoyed the joy, happiness and hope that God had to offer.

I want you to ask yourself this question, "Where am I in this story?" Do you identify with the younger son? "Give me what is mine," he said. That was the greatest insult in Middle Eastern culture. He was really saying, "Father, I want you dead." He was not entitled to his share of the estate until after the death of his father. Being the younger son his share was one-third. He took it, and he was gone. No doubt the father had to liquidate part of his estate to give the younger son a third. The younger son bought a Porsche, took off to Las Vegas and spent all of his money. He had lots of friends until his money was gone!

The Bible then says that he joined himself to a man of that far country and began feeding swine. To a Hebrew that meant that he was no longer a Hebrew but a Gentile, and he was outside the covenant. Here was a young man who was starving to death, who was shamed, who was destitute and alone and no one treated him like a human being. But then Jesus said, "He came to himself." What a marvelous statement! He came to who he really was and remembered that he was more than just someone to slop the pigs, he was a son. Once a son, always a son.

He began thinking about his father's hired servants and how much better off they were than he was, and he thought, "I will return." He practiced his speech, "Father, I have sinned against you and against the Lord. I'm not worthy to be called your son." He started home. And then in one of the tenderest moments in all of Scripture, the Bible says that the old man sitting on the front porch saw his son coming. Many times, no doubt, he had sat on that front porch, had seen a figure coming down the road and thought, "Is that him? No. It's not him." But on this day he recognized that haggard and emaciated figure and knew that it was his son. That loving prodigal father jumped from the porch and ran down the road. Aristotle said, "Men do not run in public. It is shameful for men to run in public." He ran to his son and the son tried to deliver his speech but the father said, "I don't want to hear any of that! Quick! Let's get my boy a robe and put a ring on his finger and shoes on his feet." Slaves went barefoot, but sons wore shoes. "Let's kill the fatted calf and have a party!" They had a big celebration!

Let me ask you? Would you have gone to that party? It's okay to welcome the son back, but welcome the son back to bread and water, not a party. Welcome the son back to ashes and sack cloth, not jewelry and a robe. Welcome the son back to hard work Let him prove himself. Put him on probation, let him work a while and see if he has learned his lesson. You just don't run down the road and kiss him. That's humiliating and embarrassing. I can just hear the elders at the church the following Wednesday night, "Did you see what old man so and so did? He actually ran down the road and welcomed that boy home! What kind of example is that? I'll tell you what, I hope they don't ask him to give his testimony at Reflections next Wednesday night. What kind of example is that? No responsibility. No accountability. No anything, just welcome him back. I'll tell you what, if that were my son...

Would you go to the party? They were having a party! The Bible says that the older son heard the music and the dancing. (Now I know that the dancing part is a problem for some of you. You will just have to take that up with Jesus when you get to Heaven.) The older boy heard the music. He walked up to a servant and asked what was going on. The servant needled him by saying, "Guess what, he's back, and they have killed your calf." (Can't you just imagine, he was angry and refused to go in?) He stayed on the outside, and refused his father's invitation to come to the party. Again the height of discourtesy in Middle Eastern society.

Fred Craddock, my friend and mentor, once played with the details of this story. He had the father putting the robe, shoes and ring on the older son. As he said that someone in the back of the church screamed out, "That's the way it should have been written!" We all feel that way toward the older boy to some extent. The older boy worked hard, he was faithful and loyal. He refused to go in because he was angry, resentful, judgmental and jealous. When the father heard about the older son, just as the father went to the younger son, the father went to the older son, and the older son did not give him the courtesy of calling him father. The older son said, "Look, that son of yours wasted everything. He spent it on prostitutes." Now where did he get that idea? There is nothing in the story about the man spending money on prostitutes. No! That was in the older boy's mind.

So often we project to others our own desires. The father came to his son and said, "Come in. It is needful that we make merry. Your brother was lost and is now found." He said, "Have I not always appreciated you? All I have is yours. It is needful that we have a party because your brother was lost and now is found." Where are you in this party? Are you even in the party? Where are you in the story? Do you identify with one more than the other?

In some ways I identify with the younger son and in some ways I identify with the older son. Something happened to me this past week. On Thursday First Baptist hosted a seminar on aging. I had not made any plans to attend, but I decided to walk down and talk with the guests before the seminar started. I noticed they had set up a small bookstore. I looked at the books and decided not to buy any. After mingling with some attending the seminar, for some reason I went back to the bookstore. Laying on the table was only one copy of a book by Henri Nouwen. Father Henri Nouwen, a Dutch priest who died about a year ago, is one of my favorite writers. The name of that book was *The Return of the Prodigal Son*. I knew I had to have that book and I knew I had to read it immediately.

After reading the book I said, "God, where am I in this story? What are you trying to teach me?" I didn't just stumble upon that book. I had known about that book for years. Why was it on a table for sale at an aging conference? And why was it the only one? Why did I not see it the first time, but saw it the second time? "God, what are you trying to say to me?" I'm not for sure, but maybe it is this: Sometimes I have been that younger son. I have been rebellious, bopping in and out of church every now and then, and my commitment lasting no longer than the flowers on the altar. More often I have been the older son working dutifully and faithfully but being angry and resentful. God spoke to me through that book and said, "You don't want to be either one. You want to be like the father." The father loved both of his sons. The father gave to both of his sons and the father forgave both of his sons. The father went to both of his sons. The father is the hero of the story. The prodigal father, the love-sick father, the everlasting, ever merciful, ever graceful father is just like God.

God is calling me and very possibly God is calling you to be like the father. He is calling you and He is calling me to be loving, kind, encouraging, forgiving and generous. God is calling to you and God is calling to me to be grievous over the sins and waywardness of others. How many times did that father lament and cry over both of his sons who were gone? How many times in his heart and mind did that father forgive both of his sons? How many times was that father generous to his sons? The Bible says that he literally divided his life among them. He gave them everything. He didn't condemn either one. He didn't chastise either one. He didn't ask questions of either one. He simply gave. Maybe God is calling us to be prayerful and tearful and forgiving and generous. Maybe God is calling us to be like Jesus.

I don't know where you are in this story. That's between you and God and the Holy Spirit. But I know where God wants you to be. God wants you to come home. If you are away from Him, come home. If you are in the far country, come home. If you are at home but still in the far country, come home. He wants you to come home. Softly and tenderly He is calling you to come home.

Waiting on the Porch
Luke 15:1-3, 11-32

It is about the father. It really is about the father. I know that the two sons gathered the most words in the narrative and they even gather the most of the emotions either for or against them from us when we read it. It is really about the father. I know that we have sometimes called this the parable of the prodigal son or even the parable of the two lost sons, but it is really about the father. It is about the father.

Jesus began this parable by saying a certain man had two sons. A man! That is the subject of the sentence and that is the subject of the parable. It is about the father. This prodigal father. This extravagant father. This over indulgent father. This father who loves to a fault, who forgives and forgives and forgives. This father who seeks the lost and when the lost return he welcomes them back with overindulgence and extravagance. He is an extravagant father - a prodigal father. And yes, he is an offensive father. He offends us as we read this parable. He offends our sense of fairness, of what is right and what is wrong. He offends us when we think that when you do good, you should be rewarded and when you do badly, you should be punished. No! He offends our sense of what is just and what is right. He really is a very offensive individual. He offends our sense of everything. Some things about this father we just don't like.

Now, I know you don't like the sons. That is easy. Here we have the younger son who is the one who says, "Father, give me what is mine." He disposes of it in wild living. He comes to the end of his journey and says, "I have to do something. I might as well go back to my father and become one of his hired hands." And as he is walking down the road, the haggard figure that he is, the father sees him and runs to him and kisses him and says, "Let's have a party, my son who is lost is now return." This son who is willful, selfish, self-centered, self-pitying, indulgent, and wasteful has returned and the father wants to have a party.

Then there is the older son. When the older son hears about the party he comes in and ask the servant. The servant said, "Hey, your brother is back. They are partying. "I won't go in." He becomes angry and sullen, so much so that the father has to leave the party. He comes out on the porch to find him. "Won't you come in?" "No, not with this son of yours. You have never given me a party, but yet, this son of yours comes back and you have a party for him." This older boy! The one who is petty, spiteful, jealous and utterly self-righteous. Someone has said if you want to feel sorry for someone in this parable, feel sorry for the father. He has to put up with these two spoiled brats. If anybody should have left; it should have been the father. Leave these two alone and let them fight it out for themselves. These two sons!

For you see, the younger son, when demanding what belongs to him, is actually saying to the father, "Old man, I wish you were dead." In Jewish law a son could receive his portion but he could not dispose of it until after his parent had died so really he had disposed of it before his father dies and is really saying I wish you were dead. What about that commandment which says to honor ones father and mother? And then he associates with Gentiles which is also again against Jewish custom. Then he feeds swine. Could anything be more repugnant to a Jew than that? There is the older brother. I preached a sermon one time entitled *Does the Older Brother Have a Point?* Sometimes we can almost feel empathy for this young man.

Fred Craddock preached on this and changed up some of the details of the story. He had the father taking the robe and the ring off the younger son and giving them to the older son. About that time, literally, a woman got up in the back of the church in the middle of his sermon and shouted out, "That is the way it should have been written." We feel like that just a little bit because this offends our sense of fairness. But on closer inspection we see that he addressed his father publicly with no title whatsoever, a sign of public insult. He then accuses his own father of rank favoritism and he disclaims any membership in the family. "This son of yours!" Would you want to go fishing with this guy? We do feel sorry for the father. He should have just left these two spoiled brats to themselves.

But rascals they both were. The one who was lost went away. The other was lost and stayed home. Both of them in some sense came to the father. The younger came back and asked to be one of the hired servants. The older complained to the father but when you complain to someone that you have at least some kind of sense of their own sense of right and wrong injustice. They both came back, in a sense. Why? Why do they feel a certain amount of comfort in doing so? Maybe it was because they knew that they could and that he would always be there. He was always there. The father was always there waiting on the porch, sitting on the porch, going out on the porch to bring in the other one. He was always there. It is sorta nice to know that some things are always there. But some things are not always there. I go to 3428 Madison Avenue in Gadsden, Alabama where I spent the first fifteen years of my life. The house is still there, but the garage that grandpa built is gone. It was the garage that held my first basketball goal. I spent many an afternoon trying to perfect my jump shot and playing in my imagination the end of the game scenario. You know, when the clock ticked down I would hit the long jumper as the buzzer sounded and we would win the championship. But the garage is no longer there anymore.

I go to the Southern Baptist Theological Seminary where I have spent many years of my life. I earned two degrees there. It is not there anymore. The school is still there and they have teachers and they have students, but the school that I attended is not there anymore. The distinguished faculty, the striving for excellence in theological education, not indoctrination, is not there anymore.

This coming Thursday night, Sharlon and I will go back to our home community and we will gather with a group of people and plan our fortieth high school reunion. Allen won't be there. Allen died last month. He was a member of our class. He was one of the sweetest people I have ever known in my life. He was born with severe birth defects, which led to many surgeries. He had to have medication all of his life. He died last month at fifty-eight waiting for a liver transplant. He had never touched a drop of alcohol in his life. Allen won't be there.

It was nice to know that some things will always be there. They are always there. Eddie Taylor was one of my deacons in Canaan, Indiana. He was a student at Purdue, several hundred or so miles from his home. One day he came home while a college student and stayed for thirty minutes and then went back. It was a long trip and he only stayed thirty minutes and went back. Maude, his mother, probably coming in from milking the cows without changing shoes walked into the kitchen. There she said something to Eddie's dad. "Wonder why Eddie just came home for thirty minutes?" Eddie's father probably checked to see if his false teeth were where they usually were in the front pocket of his shirt and said, "Well, Maude, don't worry about that. Worry about when he doesn't want to come home."

It is nice to know that home is always there. It is nice to know that some things are always there. God is always there. He is always there. It doesn't matter. He is always there. If you are not connected to God, it is because you moved, He didn't. If you want to find God, you go exactly back to where you lost him, because he is still there and he is still waiting for you. It is nice to know that some things are always there.

Maybe they knew instinctively, subconsciously within their own hearts that the father's nature was that of love and forgiveness and compassion. I know many of us would say, "Well, I think that younger son ought to prove himself.

That is what he ought to do. He ought to come back and get a job, get a life, grow up and prove that he is worthy, that he deserves the forgiveness that his father has shown to him. That is what he ought to do. He ought to be humble. He ought to do what is right for a change - grow up, get a job, pay some taxes, join the military or work in the church nursery. That is what he ought to do.

What about the older boy? My gracious, he needs a change of attitude, does he not? He needs to have a little bit of gratitude in his heart. His father has already promised him everything that the father owns. He inherited it all. He gained it all. It was there for him. You know his worse punishment is being who he is; the self-righteous rascal that he is. We would say that they both need to shape up and grow up. Not God! It sorta offends our sense of fairness, doesn't it? It sorta makes us wonder? Perhaps Jesus is trying to show the two groups that are listening to this: the tax collectors, the sinners, and the Pharisees. Maybe He is showing them a mirror of who they really are. You know the tax collectors and the sinners, the downtrodden of society. Then there are those religious, self-righteous Pharisees; the younger brother, and the older brother. Perhaps He is showing to them a mirror of who they really are before God. Yes that they too, sinners and Pharisees alike, need to come home to God. For you see, God is looking for those who are lost. God, who always looks for those who are lost!

Jesus also told two other parables here - the shepherd lost his sheep and went to find them and the woman loses a coin and finds it. The sheep just wander away out of stupidity. The woman loses the coin out of carelessness. It doesn't matter whether we are lost because of carelessness. It doesn't matter if we are lost because of stupidity. It doesn't matter if we are an open rebellion to God. It doesn't matter if we are in quiet defiance to God. It doesn't matter! If we are lost, God is looking for us. God is looking for you. He wants you to come home. He wants to love you. He wants to forgive you. They once asked Abraham Lincoln, "What will you do to the Southerners? How will you treat the Southerners after the war?" He said, "As if they had never left." God loves and forgives us as if we had never, ever sinned.

But not only that, He invites us to a party. The shepherd finds the sheep and rejoices, Joy is the dominant theme! The woman finds the coin. She brings her folks together and they rejoice the finding of that which is lost. The young son returns home and they have a party: Even the older brother is invited into the party. You see, throughout all of Christ's teaching, throughout the entire Bible, throughout all of what Jesus came to do and to say is this dominant theme of returning home to the loving and forgiving father. And he is throwing a party! Some people don't even know there is a party. Some people know about the party but don't think they are invited. God says to you, "There is a party going on all the time. It is called eternal life. It begins in this life and is extended into the next." He invites you to come to the party. He wants you to have a good time in His love and grace. Come on in - you honored guest!

It was September 1982, Patsy Wheat had an eight-year-old daughter and five-year-old and two-year old little boy. The two year old little boys name was Jay. She set her egg timer for ten minutes. She would do that periodically to remind herself to check on her children who were playing in the carport. The egg timer went off and she went out into the garage and found her eight-year-old and the five-year-old. She did not find the two-year-old son, Jay. He was lost. Immediately she called the police who immediately called the sheriff. Within an hour there were trucks, policemen, and at least one hundred neighbors there to help find the little boy who was lost. The father was a truck driver and was to be home about eleven o'clock that night. They looked and looked and looked. At four thirty in the afternoon the helicopters involved. About 10:30 PM that night when the father came they still had not found the little boy. About 4:30 AM someone remembered a German shepherd dog that could find people by their scent. They were able to find something that smelled of the little boy. The shepherd, after getting the scent, tore out at 4:30 AM. The shepherd began to bark. They found the dog as he had gone up the mountain and there they found the two year old little boy with his feet caught in briars, bleeding, but safe and sound. The hundreds of people who searched for him began to applaud. There was joy. There was celebration. There were tears of relief and happiness but no one was happier to see that little boy than its parent, Patsy Wheat. Oh, the love of a parent!

And oh, the love of the Father and Mother when we return home.

This loving Father is waiting for you to come home.

Believing the Bible
Luke 16:19-31

This book can change your life.

This book, the Bible, will change your life if you live it, if you read it, if you meditate upon it, if you think about it, if you let it become a part of your daily life; and if you apply it. It will change your life. It will give you hope. If you really believe the Bible; it will give you encouragement and direction for each and every decision of your life. If you really believe the Bible it will give you a purpose and meaning for life. This book can and will change one's life if we so let it. How can we read this book and it not change our life?

It reminds me of the story of the judge who was mugged. Several days later in his courtroom still wearing the bandages of the mugging made the announcement to the court in which he said, "I will not let this experience, in any way, affect my judgment in decisions of like manner in the future. A woman arose in the back of the room and said, "Mug him again!" How could you not let that kind of experience affect your decision? It is like reading the Bible. How can we read this book and it not change us? How can we meditate upon it, devour it? How can we live it and apply it and it not change who and what we are? This morning if you will hear the word of God, it could change the way you look at the poor, the destitute and the homeless. It could change the way you look at the Bible itself and how we live it and apply it to our daily lives.

Here the story. The story starts out with Jesus saying there was a rich man there always was and there always will be a rich man. There is always going to be a rich man. There is always going to be an individual who knows how to get his way in life no matter how he has to do that there was a rich man. This rich man dined sumptuously every single day in the lap of luxury. Jesus draws all of our attention to him at the beginning. True to form, to life itself, we all concentrate our mind and energy upon this rich man but, yet, there was another man in the story, a poor man. A man who had nothing, He was there but the rich man did not see him. I think the fancy term for it is habituation - we see something but we don't see it. It is there and we see it, but we don't see it. Because he had ignored or neglected the poor man so long, it got to where he did not even see the poor man.

It is sorta like today. We know that there are poor people in our world. We know that there are destitute and homeless even here in Chattanooga. We see them, but we don't see them! We have seen them so many times; we just don't see them anymore. We know that there are thirty thousand people who die every day of hunger and hunger related diseases, twenty thousand of those are children, we know that! We just don't know it. We see it, but we don't see it. We have seen it so many times, we don't see it anymore. That was true with the rich man. He saw the beggar. He just did not see him. He lived a life that was not compassionate or caring. The rich man had plenty of food. He had a lot left over and could have fed the beggar but chose not to, either because of lack of compassion or the lack of distribution. The same is true in our world today.

Jesus said that if one person eats and one person does not eat, you do not have the kingdom of God. So when both men died, one man was carried to Abraham's bosom; the other man was buried and found himself in Hades. Reversal! Radical reversal! Situations radically reversed. It was Alexander the Great who had himself buried with his arms protruding from his coffin to let everyone know that no matter how powerful or wealthy one is, we all leave this world empty handed. The rich man left this world empty handed and found himself in a situation completely opposite of that which he found himself in this world. But he is still in charge. He is still giving orders, "Father Abraham, send the water boy, Lazarus, down here to cool my tongue." Still in charge, he thinks. Father Abraham says, "Well, you know that just won't work. You remember in your life you had the best and he had nothing. Well, now that is reversed, besides you can't travel back and forth." "Well, do this for me. I have five brothers. Send him back to them." He said, "No, I can't do that either, your five brothers have the Bible, They have Moses and the prophets. They have the Bible. That is enough," "No, you don't understand, Father Abraham. If they see that He is raised from the dead that will be sensational. That will be spectacular. Then they will believe. Then they will repent." And Father Abraham said, "No! They have the Bible. They have the Bible! The Bible is enough to change their life if only they will let it.

You see the rich man was really saying that the Bible doesn't work. The Bible is not enough. "You need more than the Bible," He said, "They have the Bible that was given to them as a grammar school student by the Gideon and they have that Bible that is on the coffee table that has Grandmas old hairnet and some family recipes and they have that great big Bible that is the one we keep the family genealogy in and they even have some Bibles that they have read and are worn. But, still, the Bible is just not enough. They need more. They need something else besides the Bible, I will agree with them on one point that in some ways the Bible has been abused and it doesn't work in those kinds of situations. It does not work in situations where those have deliberately abused the Bible. If we look at the Bible in any other way except that Jesus Christ is the criterion by which all scripture is to be interpreted, it is a major negligence of the true essence of the Bible. It is misuse of the Bible. It is abuse of the Bible. It is rank heresy.

Maybe that is why we have so many groups even within Christendom who just simply use the Bible to try to sanction whatever they have already to do and to believe. I will agree there has been much abuse of God's word. I will disagree when he says that the Bible is not enough; it doesn't work. We need more than the Bible. We need something spectacular. We need something sensational. We need something that will shock them. Have somebody to be raised from the dead, and the minute they see Lazarus raised from the dead that will shock them into belief. Sad to say it has become a temptation of the church to accept that kind of philosophy. We have got to do something in the church that will shock them, that is the way you get people in the doors. Do something spectacular. Do something sensational. Do something that will shock them and then they will come. You know, do something that will draw a crowd. Have Miss America! Handle snakes I remember not to very long ago a preacher within our very own state of Tennessee wrestled a pro wrestler, He was supposed to wrestle an alligator, I think, but wound up wrestling a pro wrestler. I don't know if it made any difference, really, but he got a crowd. Do something spectacular.

I remember as a boy Homer Martinez. He was a great evangelist, who was holding a revival nearby and advertised Hot Dogs with Homer. That got all the kids there one hour before the services. There were free hotdogs, Hot dogs with Homer! It probably wouldn't work today, would it? You probably would not gather a lot of children with free hotdogs. We did in the fifties. Not today! That is what we need, we need something spectacular, something sensational that would draw a crowd, really what he was saying is that we want a miracle, we want a sign. That is what will get them there, Do something big. The Bible is not enough. Just the Bible! That is not enough.

What Jesus is saying here is that the Bible is enough. You have Moses and the Prophets in the Bible, the word of God, the living dynamic word of God, You have the Bible that bears witness to the saving grace and love of the Lord Jesus Christ. That is enough. That is enough to generate faith. It is enough to cause one to repent. It is enough to live one's life by. It is enough for one to die by and to live again by. The Bible, God's word, does work if only we will let it. It is enough if we spend fifteen or thirty minutes a day in God's word, where we meditate upon it, where we think: about it, where we study it, we do research in it, we apply it and live it in our everyday lives. How else could the Bible but work in our lives when we so very, very much let it.

It was Gandhi who said, "You Christians don't understand that you have within your possessions a book that is filled with dynamite. It could blow civilization to bits. It could turn society upside down and it could bring peace to a war torn world and you read it like it is a piece of literature." This book is alive and the Jesus Christ, to whom its witness, and is its very center is alive and active just as much as He has ever been in the history of our planet and it is through this book that we learn about Him and the Bible will live if only we will let it There is a marvelous new area of Biblical criticism today called Rhetorical Criticism which simply says that we can't waste time. The need is too urgent! We can't waste time trying to figure out if the world was created four thousand four years ago. God knows that we don't! We can't worry about whether the whale swallowed Jonah or Jonah swallowed the whale, we can't worry about whether every little aspect of archeological research and Biblical criticism matches up with Darwinism. How much effort and time have we spent over questions for which there are no eternal answers? There are eternal answers in the Bible, We need to center our minds, Rhetorical Criticism says, on letting this book change your life. It's been around over two thousand years and it will be around two thousand more years, if the Lord does not come again.

Let this book change your life. It has been doing it for thousands of years. It has withstood every criticism and every attempt to hide it and burn it in the history of our planet. It will always stand, Jesus said, "My word shall stand forever." Isn't that exciting? We need to quit wasting time asking questions that no one is asking and let this book live and let this book live through us. That is why it is still important to study the Bible. It is still important to have a Sunday School class where we meet every week and study God's word, have small groups like Companions in Christ and Kerygma classes where we study God's word. It is important to have Bible Study in the homes in groups or personal Bible study. That is why Bible study still is very, very at the center of whom and what we are as Christians. If only we will believe it. If only we will live it.

I was lucky and I know that many of you were lucky to have a home in which the Bible was read. I was taught to memorize scripture. "The Lord is my shepherd, I shall not want. He maketh me to lie down in green pastures."(Psalm 23: 1-2a) "In my father's house are many mansions and if it were not so I would have told you." "I go and prepare a place for you and if I go and prepare a place for you then I will come again and receive you unto myself." (John 14:3) "Jesus is the truth, the way and the life." (John 14:6) He cares for you. "God is love." You have your favorite verses, too. They are not just in this book. They are in your heart and in your life. You live by them each and every day. You see this book will change our life if we will set before it and let the Holy Spirit guide us. This book will change our life if we will look at this book with an open mind. Not like we already know what it means, because we may not, but with a naiveté, a freshness, let this book speak to us. And with a receptive heart not only to hear what the scripture says but let that word dwell in our hearts so we might not sin against God. That it might be a guide to our daily life, a lamp unto our feet, and a light unto our path.

Let God's spirit, the one who originally inspired the Bible, interpret these words to us. Always remembering that the heart and center and witness of this book is Jesus Christ; His word, His character, His personality, His spirit, His love, His grace, His mercy. This book is about Jesus. It is not about anything else. It is about Jesus and His love for you and me and the way Jesus wants to change our life and as we live our life in a personal relationship with Jesus Christ this book will change your life. If we are not personally aligned with the Lord Jesus Christ we cannot understand what this book says. He is at its heart. He is at its center. The Bible is enough to generate faith, purpose, meaning, hope, forgiveness, and love in our lives.

"It is not enough," He said. We need a sign. We need something spectacular, sensational. No the Bible is enough. Does that mean that we should never have anything sensational or spectacular? Does that mean that our worship should not be energetic and have emotion and feeling and be something that is contagious and lifts up the name of the Lord with energy? No! It should always be that way. Sometimes our worship should be inspirational. Sometimes our worship should cause us to be lifted up high emotionally and come to God with praise and adoration. Does that mean that we should never have miracles? Of course not. God is still as much a God of miracles as ever He was. God has not quit doing miracles. He is just as much miraculous today as He was when Jesus walked this earth.

Look around you. Each and everyday things happen for which there is no other explanation except God, himself. That is a miracle. They happen everywhere. People see them everywhere if only they have eyes to see and ears to hear. Does that mean we should not have signs? Of course not. Signs are everywhere. Look at the beauty of God's world. Look at the love in the face of a parent for a child, a grandparent for a grandchild, a husband for a wife, a friend for a friend, a Christian for a Christian. God's signs are everywhere. Everywhere! I received a sign myself. Just a couple of weeks ago I stood in this very pulpit and preached from the parable of the persistent widow who said time and time again, "We must persist. We must pray." We must persistently perseveringly pray and never give up. At the end of the service Steve Dawson came up to me and said, "Do you remember that story about Winston Churchill and the most famous speech he ever gave?" Winston Churchill was standing before a graduating class, paused and then said, "Never. Never. Never give up!" And then he sat down. It was the most memorable speech he ever gave. Those words haunted me all day long. That night I was faced with a very crucial decision about someone I cared very deeply. I found myself in Gadsden, Alabama about one o'clock in the morning about to get on the interstate facing a decision and I did not know what to do. As I got off the highway and onto the interstate there was a billboard. I had never seen it before, and on that billboard was a picture of Winston Churchill. He was pictured there with both fingers in the victory sign and said, "Never! Never! Never give up!"

Coincidence? I don't think so. It was a sign from God, but please remember it started with Jesus and the Bible.

I Wanna Big Faith
Luke 17:5-10

The drive home from the doctor's office was lonely, but she didn't mind. It gave her a chance to pray, and she prayed, "Oh, Lord, I knew that the cancer had returned. The doctor only affirmed what I already felt. Now I'm really going to need you, Lord. I need faith, Lord, to help prepare my family. Lord, you have helped me to make my life mean something. Help me to make my death, mean something. Help me, Lord. I need you, Lord. Thank you, Lord. I know that you will not let me down."

He always paid the bills, but this time he found himself elbow deep in bills. It seemed like everything had gone up. The property taxes were up. The insurance was up. Everything seemed to be up. As he wrote his tithe check, he looked at it and thought to himself, "Lord, this is a commitment that I have made to you. Give me the faith to keep it."

She didn't sleep at all. She got up earlier than usual and as always she had her devotional time first thing. It always got her day off on the right foot. And wouldn't you know it, as she read the Bible lesson assigned for that day from her devotional book, she read the words in Luke 17:4, "If he sins against you seven times a day and seven times comes back to you and says, 'I repent,' forgive him." She said, "Lord, did you say seven times in one day? I couldn't forgive him once all night. He has lied to me again! He has controlled me! He has manipulated me! And you want me to forgive him again? Lord that is going to demand more faith than I've got. I need more faith, Lord."

Now you understand how the disciples and why the disciples were able to say, "I wanna big faith. Increase my faith, Lord." Jesus had just told them, "If your brother sins against you seven times in one day and asks for forgiveness seven times, you forgive him seven times." He said on other occasions, "Seventy times seven." And the disciples cried out, "Lord, if we're going to have to do that we need more faith. This is too much for me! 'I cannot handle that! This is more than I can do in my own strength." The disciples sometimes are portrayed in the New Testament as sort of slow.

In fact, most of the time they are seen as a bunch of dullards who never got what Jesus was talking about. In fact, they never really understood Jesus until after the resurrection, but you've got to give them their due in this situation. After hearing what Jesus had just told them, they were very insightful and said, "Lord, if we're going to have to do that we need more faith than we already have. We cannot do that." The disciples were insightful in seeing that faith was something growing dynamic. Faith is something that is alive and faith is something you can grow in and faith, real faith, can only come as a gift from God, and the disciples realized that.

But more than that the disciples realized that Jesus was calling them as Christians to live to a higher standard. Jesus does not call us to be good people, Jesus calls us to be Christian people. Jesus does not call us to be good workers, He calls us to be Christian workers. Jesus does not call us to be good leaders, He calls us to be Christian leaders. Jesus does not call us to be good parents, He calls us to be Christian parents. Jesus doesn't call us to be good marriage partners, He calls us to be Christian marriage partners. Jesus calls us to live to a higher standard. Jesus calls us to live not as people who are just good people who keep their word but Christian people who keep their word.

Jesus was calling the disciples and He calls us to live our lives to a higher standard, not just a good standard. We are to live our lives to the standard of Jesus, Himself No wonder they cried out, "Lord, if we're going to have to do that, we're going to have to have more faith than we already have." But then Jesus threw them a curve ball. He said, "Wait a minute. You don't need more faith. You just need to exercise the faith that you already have." Jesus started out by saying, "If you have faith (the actual translation says, 'You do.') the size of a mustard seed..." A mustard seed is the size of the head of a pin and if you have just that small amount of faith, you can do great things because you are dealing with a God who does the impossible, and you just need a little bit of faith.

Every single person in this congregation today has faith. You had faith when you sat down that the pew would not fall under you. You have faith as you sit here that the ceiling is not going to fall on your head. You have faith that I'm going to preach a short sermon and you're going to be out by twelve 0' clock. (Sometimes it might not work.) You already have faith. When you get a sore throat, you go to a doctor who cannot write. He or she gives you a piece of paper and you take it to a pharmacist whose name you do not know. The pharmacist gives you a medicine you cannot pronounce and, yet, you take it thinking that you are going to get better. You have faith. We don't need more faith, we need simply to exercise the faith that we already have. Faith in the biblical concept is not the adherence to a creed. It is not belief in a certain set of doctrines. It is not ail emotion or an inner feeling. Faith is something that we act upon. It is action. Action!!

It was Ralph Sockman who said that many people are waiting around for God to do something for them instead of with them. God wants to do something with you and me as we exercise our faith, and we already have enough faith. JUST USE IT! There was a seeker of truth who went to a woman who was known for her devotion and piety. He wanted to learn the secrets of her spiritual life. He said, "I understand that you are a woman of great faith." She said, "No, my son, I am not. I am a woman of little faith in a great God." Jesus said, "You already have faith." All you need is mustard seed faith and with the God of the impossible you can do anything.

Then Jesus told a parable. Now, agreed, it is not one of our favorite parables, in fact, Edwin Steimile once read it from the Bible as the text for his sermon and a preacher jumped up in the back of the congregation and said, "Jesus never said that!" Yes, He did! So let us listen to this difficult parable and try to see what He is saying to us today. Jesus said, "Suppose one of you had a servant plowing or looking after the sheep, would he say to the servant when he comes in from the field, 'Now you just come along and sit down to eat.' Now the master says to the servant. You prepare my meal and then after I have eaten then you can eat." After all isn't that what servants do? Servants serve. Tough word.

What is Jesus saying? I'm not for sure I know, but maybe He is saying that sometimes we exercise our faith simply through duty, the kind of duty that you do when you are already dead tired. We exercise our faith through duty when we've already put in a hard day. We exercise our faith through duly when we've done it a hundred times before. We exercise our faith through Christian duty simply because nobody else will do it and we're the only ones who will do it.

Maybe Jesus is just simply saying that we exercise our faith through the duty of doing what servants always do and servants serve. We don't congratulate a fish because it swims. We don't congratulate a bird because it flies. You don't congratulate a servant because a servant serves. That's what servants do. When we signed up to be servants of the Lord Jesus Christ, we knew what we were getting into. The job description is: servants of the Lord Jesus Christ serve. You can't run a church without duty bound Christians who come here Sunday after Sunday, Wednesday after Wednesday and simply do the job. They turn on, turn off the lights. They take care of the babies in the nursery. They drive the buses. They do all of these little menial tasks that are great tasks because without them you cannot run a church. We need those clock and calendar Christians. You put it on the calendar, they put it on their clock and they will be there. They are the Martha's that work sometimes out of pure duty or out of habit. And this world cannot function without them. They do it without fanfare. They do it without a "that a boy." They do it without a headline. They do it without a plaque or trophy. They just do it because that's what servants do. Servants serve! They don't do it for reward.

Aren't you tired of these text book testimonies? You've heard the testimony that always goes something like this: "I was rich. I was powerful. I had everything. I had a beautiful wife. I had lots of money. I started drinking, then I got on drugs and started running around on my wife. I was down and out and then I found Jesus. Now I have lots of money. I have lots of power and I have a prettier wife than I had before. Ain't God good?" It don't always work that way, does it? It ain't necessarily so.

When a servant serves the Lord Jesus Christ, it is without expectation of reward. We do it because that is what we signed up to do. We do it because that is what we are called to do. We're servants and we exercise our faith by doing what servants are called to do. Even though it may be duty bound, sometimes it may be purely out of habit and sometimes it may be simply because no one else will do it. Sometimes we rise to that higher standard which says we do what we do because we love the Lord Jesus Christ. That is the higher standard He calls us to. He calls us to serve not just out of duty, not just for reward but simply because we love the Lord Jesus.

The Malaki Leper Colony is renowned for its work with the lepers. It was said that a party of British people, distinguished people, society people were touring the leper colony, and there one of 'the proper and prim ladies saw a nun down on her hands and knees in the dirt of the leper colony binding the ugly, horrible grotesque bloody wounds of the leper. That woman looked at that scene and in repulsion she said, "I wouldn't do that for ten-thousand dollars." The nun looked up at her and said, "I wouldn't either." Some things we do simply not out of reward or even out of habit but every now and then we are able to rise up to a higher standard and do something because we love the Lord Jesus.

Robert Cole, that great Harvard professor, has written a new book, *The Call to Service*. He is interested in why people do what they do. He interviewed a lot of different people who spend their lives helping and serving other people, and he asked them this question: "What are you getting out of this?" And almost to the person they would say, "Well, I really don't know." But he said almost to the person they responded that at least one time in their life they had an encounter with an individual who was not selfish and self-absorbed, a person who was not interested in all they could grab, a person who laid it all on the line, a person who was giving and unselfish and set an example for them, and they wanted to be like that person. Wouldn't it be great to be just like Jesus? Can you think of anything in this world any more wonderful than being like our Lord Jesus? "Exercise your faith," He said, "you've got enough faith, exercise it."

The crops were wilted. The small village had been without rain for a long period of time. This was an agricultural community that was about to lose their livelihood. The elders, the spiritual leaders of the community said, "As a village we're going to gather on the town square this coming Lord's Day and devote an entire hour to prayer for rain. The people came. They brought objects of their faith. Some brought holy books, some brought rosaries, and some brought crosses and others objects of their faith. As they gathered around and prayed in earnest for a solid hour and it was as if by magic the heavens opened and soft drops of rain began falling, and then they learned the greatest lesson from a nine year old girl who walked among the crowd with an umbrella. She was the only one who brought an umbrella.

When You are About to Quit
Luke 18:1-8

During the month of January, I will be preaching Sunday mornings, Sunday evenings and Wednesday evenings from texts that are found only in the Gospel of Luke. Luke gives a marvelous portrait of Jesus, our Lord. Luke is a wonderful preacher in fashioning and molding and presenting the life and works of Jesus in a way that speaks to those who hear and read his words.

Every time I preach I try to fashion and form the experience of the biblical text to where it applies to our everyday life, and I hope as we study these selected texts that you will see not only what a great preacher Luke was. But what a wonderful Saviour to whom he witnesses.

Luke is very helpful in helping us to understand the Scriptures. In our Scripture text today Luke tells us why Jesus told this parable. Luke says in verse 1 that Jesus told his disciples a parable to show them that they should always pray and not give up. We are to always pray. We are to persevere and be persistent in prayer. We should never give up.

Luke tells the story of an unjust judge, a man who feared neither men nor the law and a man who was not a foreigner to bribes, and of a poor helpless widow. In Jesus' day the most helpless person in society was a widow. She not only had lost her husband; she had lost her means of support, often having to resort to begging or to the streets. She had no one to speak for her. She was always in mourning and was always wearing the clothes of mourning. But this widow would not be denied. She persisted. She would not give up; continually silo kept going back to the judge and even an unjust judge, an anti-hero if you will. Even he listened to her and granted her justice because of her persistence.

What is Jesus saying? Is Jesus saying that God is like that? Of course not! This is a parable of contrast, not a parable of comparison. He is saying if an unjust judge who cares neither about law or men will grant Justice because of persistence how much more will God grant love to those He loves and how much more will He hear the prayers of those for whom He cares. A marvelous parable!

Evidently there were those in Jesus' day who were ready to give up. There were those who were weary of praying and Jesus was saying to them, "Hang in there. Don't quit! Keep on going because... "Why did Jesus say continue to pray, keep on praying, persevere, keep on seeking, asking, knocking?

Maybe it was because perseverance in prayer creates within us a certain discipline.

I remember as a small boy asking my father that if I ate everything on my plate would I be grown the next day. He said, "Of course, not!" It's not that easy, is it? Growing up is a process that takes time and requires a certain amount of discipline, and that is also true spiritually. Many young adults experience a certain amount of frustration and disillusionment when they cannot start out their independent life at the stage of their parents. They fail to realize that it took their parents twenty to twenty-five years to get where they are.

They tell us that the professional body builders will spend weeks and weeks, sometimes months to add only one-half inch to a muscle, and certainly the development of spiritual muscles takes time. It is a process that takes discipline. Longfellow said, "The heights by great men reached and kept were not attained by sudden flight. But they while their companions slept were toiling upward in the night."

Persistence in prayer creates within us a certain spiritual discipline whereby we develop our own spiritual muscles, but it also helps to create and develop in us character. You don't hear a lot about real character today. I don't know how to define it. Maybe I'm talking about kindness and just common decency, and Integrity and respect for other people and their feelings. It just seems to me that character would encompass some of those things, and we find some of those characteristics lacking today.

We live in a world where publicly people criticize each other and call each other names. People get rich making fun of other people on television and radio. I'm not just talking about recent events ln our news. I'm talking about an overall spirit of meanness. One of making fun and calling people names and ridiculing publicly people who cannot and will not defend themselves. It's a little bit sick if you ask me. If you were to talk about a gentlemen's agreement in our society there are some who would laugh. What about real character? What about real integrity? I think persistence in prayer helps to create that and gives to us a quiet center of strength from which to live our lives.

One of the greatest honors I have ever had in the ministry was being asked to serve on the Executive Secretary Search Committee that called Dr. Earl Potts to the highest position that Alabama Baptists have. I had never heard or seen so much politicking in all of my life. People called me, calling me their long lost brother and I didn't even know their name. People had wonderful suggestions for me who just a few days earlier didn't even know my name. Politics like you wouldn't believe. After a yearlong process it came time for the recommendation. Many people gathered as the recommendation was to be presented. There was this group and that group forming all kinds of meetings trying to get their candidate elected. One group had a substitute motion to the committee's motion. Everybody was ready to attack. When the recommendation was given for Dr. Earl Potts, a quiet hush fell over the room. It was like the entire situation was defused. All the ammunition was tossed out the window and even his predecessor who had campaigned for one year for someone else had to admit with a smile, "He has a sweet spirit." And he was elected unanimously.

I'm talking about morality and integrity that is so indicative of a person that even those who would disagree with them have to respect their integrity. Whoever said that character has to be paraded in an ego that always has to be - in the spotlight? Whoever said that real leadership and real integrity has to be controlling and manipulative and autocratic? Whoever said that we have to be so insecure that we can never let anyone else be strong? Whoever said that real character and integrity cannot come from a quiet and decent center of one's life? Is that not the way that Jesus lived His life?

It was Vince Lombardi who said that a crisis does not create character it only displays it. Jesus said that character is created in the prayer closet and gives to us that quiet center of compassion and conviction that causes us to live our lives with a caring for other people with honesty and integrity. And that is found through prayer. Persistence through prayer not only creates in us a discipline, it not only creates in us a character and is a demonstration of our faith.

How easy it is to have faith when the shelves are full, the stomach is satisfied, the answers to prayer are rolling in, and everybody is happy and healthy. What about those times when the answers aren't coming and when the heavens seem so strangely silent and the shelves are empty and the coffers are empty and the stomach is hungry? Jesus said that you pray and still you pray and still you pray. That's faith!

It is faith when she sits at her Christmas Eve breakfast table and there is an empty chair and the loneliness is so great and her heart hurts so bad that she cannot stand it but still she prays. Faith is when that hulking six foot, three, two-hundred-twenty-five pounds of a man stands over the casket of a daughter and cries so deeply that he has to be helped back to his chair by his wife. But still he prays. That's faith. That's faith. It's when it is difficult to pray that we pray and still we pray and we persist and we persevere and we just keep on praying.

Evelyn Newman tells of an experience. When things would get rough she would go to the lake behind her small mountain cabin. She loved to walk along the side of the lake and see the reflection of the mountains and just adore the beauty of the still lake. During one troubled time, she went to the lake and the winds were blowing, and the water was brisk. As she was looking out over the lake, it occurred to her that even God cannot paint a portrait on moving water.

You want character; you want discipline; you want faith, stop and pray.

Press On!
Luke 18:1-8

This morning I want to talk about asking God for stuff, I want to talk about asking for stuff. Jesus, according to Luke, tells us that we should, must, ought to pray always and never, ever give up.

Now that is a little bit of an unusual attack because Jesus usually, not always, but usually takes the inductive approach. He sorta presents the situation and leaves the conclusion and the subsequent action to the individual. Very rarely does Jesus fill the air with ought, must and should. Usually it is more of an engagement of the personality helping them to work through and come to their own conclusion, and hopefully, to their own action. That is true most always. You remember the lawyer comes to Jesus and says, "Who is my neighbor?" Jesus tells him the parable of the Good Samaritan and says, "Now who do you think is your neighbor?"

It happened when the cantankerous people brought the woman caught in adultery, threw her at the feet of Jesus and said, "Now the law says that she should be stoned. What do you think?" Jesus said, "Any of you who are without sin yourself start picking up some rocks." Leaving to them their own guilt and conviction.

Even there are times when Jesus said you must do something. You should do something. As with Nicodemus - you must be born again. As to the rich young ruler - you have to take what you have and give it to the poor. Still Jesus left the decision with the individual. He used the inductive approach rather than take the deductive - ought, must and should. This is what you do and you should to do it. You ought to do it. You must do it. You have to do it now. However, with this statement there is no option. There is no alternative. There is no either, or, if, but, or should. This is it. This is the way it should be. This is the way it has to be: you ought to always, you should always, and you must always pray and never, ever give up.

Jesus says it as adamantly through the words of Luke as ever He said anything. You ought to pray. Pray! That is what He is talking about. Talking with God. Listening to God. Nothing fancy. Nothing that you have to have a list of degrees for, just pray. Talk with God. Listen to God. He doesn't say read a book on prayer. He says pray. He doesn't say enter into a conversation about prayer. He says pray. He doesn't say attend a lecture on prayer. He says pray. He doesn't say lead a philosophical discussion on the rudiments of prayer. He says simply, "Pray." Talk to God! Spend time with God. Nurture your relationship to God.

We spend time and energy with the people that we love and really care for. If we really care for a person, we stay in contact with that person, do we not? We talk to that person. We give to them our time and our energy. We love them. One way that we show our love to an individual is by staying in touch with them and giving to them our attention. In fact the worst form of hatred is to ignore someone. How much do we love God if we ignore him? How much do we love God if we talk to him? As we talk to Him and nurture our relationship with Him, we begin to develop the character that God has.

It is true, is it not, that we take on the character and personality traits of people with whom we spend the most time. They become more like us and we become more like them. It is true with God. If we really spend time with God, get into God, then we become more and more like God. His characteristics become our characteristics. His nature becomes our nature. His personality becomes ours because we are with Him all the time. We pray! We pray all the time. We pray about everything. We simply talk to God.

Many of you as a parent or grandparent have read the little children's book called *The Bernstein Bears Get the Gimmes*. There is a marvelous scene in the story where brother and sister are begging mother in the store for some little toy that sticks out its tongue. They just continue to beg. "Gimme, Gimme, gimme! Please! Please! Please mamma! Finally mamma says, "Now hush! That is enough." The children continue to pursue and finally the father says, 'This is the most outrageously embarrassing behavior." It seems that brother and sister have the galloping, greedy, gimmes.

We are sorta like that, aren't we? Most of us some of the time; some of us most all the time have a case of the galloping, greedy gimmes. Gimme! Gimme! I want more. I just want more. What happens when we spend time with God and we develop in ourselves God-like characteristics? God takes that basic self-serving characteristic or trait and begins to turn it around into something good. This desire for gimme, gimme, gimme can become a persistent pursuing within us of generosity and gratitude toward others. God takes something that is selfish and self-centered within our lives and turns it into something that is outwardly generous and extravagantly great. That is what happens with God. He helps to change us as we spend more and more time with him. He takes our case of the gimmes and turns it into a persistence in prayer that helps to develop God-like characteristics in our own life. For you see that is why Jesus said, "Pray. We should pray and pray always." Jesus said in the Sermon on the Mount that we should keep on asking. We should keep on seeking. We should keep on knocking.

Paul says that we should pray without ceasing. Luke, here in his own words, describing the parable says we should pray and pray always. Pray in everything. Pray in good times and in bad. Maybe God is just waiting on us to see if we are serious about this. Are we really serious about this matter? When we ask God for stuff are we really serious about it or is just some flippant desire? Or is it just the whim of the second? Or is it something about which we really are serious? Is it something about which we deeply care? Is it something about which we have a passion? What are you passionate about in your own spiritual life? We pray about that which we care and about which we are passionate.

It was Fred Craddock who tells about the African American Pastor who says, "Do not talk to me about prayer until you have stood at a locked door for years with bloody knuckles." That is the kind of persistent, persevering prayer that Jesus is talking about. As we persevere in that kind of prayer it then begins to condition us that we might be able to receive that which God already wants to give us. God loves us. God cares for us. He wants to give you everything you need to accomplish His will, but sometimes He has to wait because we are not conditioned to receive it. I can pray for the wisdom of God. "God give me your wisdom." But unless I am prepared to receive it, it would be like trying to put a baby grand piano into a broom closet. Maybe we are just not ready to receive it. We have not conditioned ourselves to receive it. We have to meet the requirements to receive it.

We can pray until we are blue in the face about forgiveness but unless we have forgiven others we are not going to find it. The Bible clearly states that unless we have forgiven others, God cannot forgive us. We can pray all day long for forgiveness, but if we hold unforgiveness in our own hearts we have not met God's requirements. So, you see, maybe He is waiting for us to do what we need to do to become receptive. Or maybe He is waiting to see what we would do with it if He did grant our request. I can pray for power and authority, but God is not going to give it to me if I am going to use it for my own selfish purposes. Why should He? I could pray for the opportunities of life, but if I am not going to use that for His kingdoms work, if I am not going to use that to make people better to give people a better place to live then why should He give it to me in the first place. Maybe God is waiting on us to see how we would use those gifts if He were to give them to us. Pray! And when we have that kind of persistence it is a way of conditioning our own self to receive that which God already wants to give to us and then we will be ready to receive it and to use it as He wants it to be used.

All day long, every day in millions of areas of the world there is a confrontation between the stream and the rock. The stream is liquid water. The rock is a solid mass. It seems like very little is changing but over a period of time, without exception, that confrontation between the stream and the rock, the stream will always win. Always! It might take a long time, but that stream with its unrelenting flow will eventually wear down the rock. It can carve out the Grand Canyon. It always wins! It is true persistent prayer. It will always win to accomplish God's goal. So, we pray and we pray always about everything and anything and we never ever give up. That is the point of the parable. Because here is this persistent widow who keeps bothering this immoral and unjust judge. She just wears him out, literally. And then he finally states, "I don't care about her or anybody else or even justice, but because she keeps on pestering me I will grant her wish. I will give to her what she already deserves and that is justice."

You wonder sometime if the reason we don't receive justice for ourselves is that we are not willing to grant it to others. But she did! She received justice. Remember this is not a parable of comparison. God is not the unjust judge. In fact this woman is sorta a un-hero herself. It is not a parable of comparison. It is a parable of contrast and Jesus is using what He uses so many times. If an immoral, uncaring; uncompassionate, unjust judge will grant a request, how much more will God. How much more would someone who wants the very, very best for you, who wants nothing better for you than to see His will accomplished; how much more will God give to you. That is what he wants to do. And in us that kind of persistent pestering produces faith. It is said in verse eight, "When the son of man comes, will he find this kind of faith on the earth?" And he looks to us and says, "Is that your kind of faith?" The kind of faith that continually, perseveringly, persistently with endurance goes to God. Even when the heavens seem silent. Even when the people who are the point of our prayers seem unfazed. Even when the problems do not seem to be getting better, only worse. But still we pray. We pray! In faith we pray. Because we know that in the end, whether God gives to us the things for which we are praying whether it be small or huge it doesn't matter. He always gives the best gift He can give. He always, without exception, answers our prayer with the very, very best gift that He can give. He always gives to us, himself.

No matter what the problem, no matter what the situation, no matter what kind of stuff we are praying for if we pray, pray always and never quit. He gives to us his most precious gift. He gives to us, Himself.

She was trapped in an elevator. It was a horrible position for anyone, but particularly for one who is claustrophobic. They ask her from the outside, "Are you alone?" She replies, "I am by myself, but I am not alone." We are never alone as His child. No matter what the situation. No matter how silent the heavens may seem. No matter how dark the trouble may be, we are never, ever alone and we should never, ever quit praying. The farmer saw the sparrow lying on his back. The farmer looked at the sparrow and said, "Why are you in this upside down position?" The sparrow answered back, "Well, I heard that today the sky would fall." The farmer laughed and said, "And you with those little, bitty, skinny legs are going to hold up the sky." And the sparrow said, "One does what one can." And that is all that anybody can do, but we can always without exception pray. Always and never, ever quit. Why don't we pray right now?

It's Not About Me!
Luke 18:9-14

Jay Wallace Hamilton was a great preacher of a generation ago. He wrote several wonderful books including one entitled *Ride the Wild Horses*. In one of the chapters he talks about the drum major instinct. He says that we all want to feel important. We all want to surpass others. We all want to excel and succeed. As Carl Sandburg said, "Everyone wants to play Hamlet," Hamilton said, "We all want to lead a parade." Hearing and reading that, I was reminded when I was in the seventh grade and we used to all go to the football games, not because the football team was very good. In fact they were very, very poor but the band was wonderful. The Emma Samson High School Marching Band were National Champions and everyone would go to watch the half-time show. Leading that half-time show was the drum major, who was eight feet tall and weighed one hundred pounds and had a hat all that was another four feet high. He would lead the band onto the field and he was a show. He would prance down the field with his knees coming up to his chin, his arms waving in the air and balancing that baton; he was something to see.

I remember one particular half-time show when he was strutting down the field like nobody's business, knees up to his chin, arms waving, leaning back just as far as he could. You can guess what happened. He fell right all his back right there in front of everybody in the stadium.

It sorta reminded me of the story they tell about the young arrogant preacher. He had it all down pat. He was so full of himself and was going to show them. He was really going to tell the folks on that day and so he struts up to the pulpit with a smirk on his face and prissiness to his air and is going to let them have it and you can guess what happened. He forgot his sermon. He mumbled and stumbled and then finally he left the pulpit with his head down humiliated and shameful. As he made his way out of the church an elderly lady in the congregation said to him, "Young man if you had gone in the way you came out; you would have come out the way you went in."

It is sorta like the dynamic we see in the parable that Jesus tells in the 18th chapter of the Gospel of Luke. It is a parable about two men who went to pray. One was a man esteemed in society and his prayer was not heard. The other was 'a scoundrel and his prayer was heard. It was a reversal of values; 'the upside down values of the Kingdom of God, surprise, an interesting dynamic. You see last Sunday we talked about the parable of the persistent widow. We talked about if one persists in their prayer life and does not give up. "Never, never, never give up!" says Jesus and Winston Churchill. If we do not give up then that kind of persistent prayer conditions us to receive the answers that God wishes to give to us. What are those conditions? What is the condition that leads us to pray correctly and to receive the answers that God wishes for us to have. Well, it wasn't like the Pharisee. The Pharisee said, "It is about me. It's about me!" He got in a prominent place in the Temple and Jesus said he prayed about himself. That he did not pray to God. He prayed about himself, and to himself, and begins this self-congratulations, "I thank you God that I am not like this other person and that I fast twice a week and that I tithe." These are good things, but what was wrong with his prayer? First of all I think it was comparative. He was putting himself in a position to look down upon someone else. It is true, I think, that we can always find someone to whom we can compare ourselves favorably. We can always find someone in our own insecurity to look down upon and feel superior to them. That is what he did. He compared his estate to the estate of the tax collector and felt superior about himself. We can always find someone to whom we can compare ourselves favorably.

I will never forget when I was a junior in high school taking physics. That was the first mistake. The first six weeks I did not get a good grade. In fact I got a "D". I was going to have to figure out how I was going to tell my parents so when I came home with that "D" on my report card I said, "Dad, did you know old Pebble?" His name was Ronald Stone. We called him Pebble. "Did you know that Pebble got an 'F' in physics? Yes, Pebble got an 'F' in Physics. What about that? Pebble got an 'F' in Physics." He said, "Well, what did you get?" I said, "Did I tell you that Pebble got an 'F' in Physics?" He said, "Well, what did you get?" "Well, I got a 'D.' Did I tell you that Pebble got an 'F' in Physics" And Dad said, "Did anybody get an 'A'?"

You see, we can always find someone with whom we can compare ourselves favorably. And oh, how we like to look down upon others. The problem is we do not want to look up. We do not want to compare ourselves to the one to whom we should be comparing ourselves and that is Jesus. You see, Jesus always got an "A" no matter what we get. He always got an "A" and we need to compare ourselves to him. Maybe that was part of the problem. Maybe part of the problem also with the man who said it's about me, is that he was looking only at the externals of what he had done on the outside and not looking at what he was on the inside. He tried to justify himself. Isn't it amazing how much time we spend trying to justify ourselves - making excuses for what we do, trying to make it look legitimate, comparing it to someone else. How much time do we waste in a silly, silly way trying to justify ourselves? Because you see this man's attitude had distorted his own view of himself, the tax collector, and even of God, Himself. It had distorted and caused him to be simply full of pride. Full of pride!

You remember the story of the pastor who came to pray in the Sanctuary every morning. He began to pray the prayer "I am nothing. I am nothing. I am nothing." Well, the associate pastor heard that and he thought that was a pretty good thing. So, every morning he began to join the pastor and they both prayed, "I am nothing. I am nothing. I am nothing." Well, the church custodian saw that and he thought that might be a good thing as well. So he too began to pray and on his first time at praying so the pastor punched the associate pastor and said, "Look who thinks he is nothing."

You see there can even be a pride about our humility. It's about me! The Pharisee said, "It's about me." The tax collector said, "It is not about me. It is not about me." He would not even stand in a prominent place. Over to the side he went. He would not even look heavenward, smote his breast and said, "God be merciful unto me a sinner." This prayer has become known as the peasant's prayer, one of the most famous prayers ever to be prayed for two thousand years in Christendom. A simple beautiful kingdom prayer - God be merciful unto me, a sinner. He was able to pray so because he had an honest, realistic appraisal of himself, not a condescending attitude toward someone else, not a looking up to someone else in admiration or inferiority, but an honest appraisal of who he was. You see, in the Bible the word confess means to say the same. Before you can confess you have to see yourself the same as does God. That was where he began. He saw himself not as others did but as God did. He had an authentic honest appraisal of himself and that in essence caused him to respond in confession and repentance, "Lord, be merciful unto me a sinner."

They say that an ego and an egg are both the same in that to be worth a flip they have to be broken. It is not about me! It is not about me. It is about an attitude of honest appraisal of ourselves, realistically seeing who we are as we compare ourselves to the one who always made an "A". We raised three sons. Sometimes I felt we were raising four. We had Chris, Brad and Scott and sometimes I felt there was a fourth son in our household by the name of Not Me. Because anytime something happened "not me" was the response. "Well, who broke it?" "Not me! Not me! Not me!" "Who did it?" There would be a chorus of "not me." We don't want to say it's me. We do not want to say I did it. We would rather say it is about me and my self-centeredness.

It is a true story. Habitat for Humanity is such a marvelous organization. It has done so much good throughout the world. It was told that recently a house was to be completed. The next day it was not quite completed. During the night the project manager saw a light in the house and heard someone in the house at two o'clock in the morning. He walked into the house and there was one of the workers on his hands and knees in the kitchen laying tile at two in the morning. "What are you doing, man?" He said, "Well the family is to move in tomorrow. I do not want them disappointed. They need to have this house completed. It needs to be complete, warm and welcoming." The man upon his hands and knees at two o'clock in the morning laying kitchen tile was the former President of the United States, Jimmy Carter. It is not about me!

That pretty much has been the place where we end most of the sermons on the parable of the two men who went to pray. That is pretty much the traditional approach and we have used it to sorta bash the Pharisee in his hypocrisy and his self-centeredness. We have used it sorta to exalt the tax collector his humility, and his lack of pride. But if we end the story there we are selling it far short of what our Lord intended when He told the story. For you see to be honest with you, the Pharisee was the best of the best. If there was an upstanding person in the community it was the Pharisee. If there was anyone who went to church regularly, who treated his family wonderfully, who gave to the support of the church, it was the Pharisee. The Pharisee was the one who paid the salaries of the preachers who preached and condemned the Pharisee. He was the best of the best.

And to be honest with you the tax collector was the worst of the worst. He was a scoundrel. He was a traitor and more than likely he was a thief. He lived off of misery and cheated others. I mean it is hard to tell who the good guys are and who the bad guys are in this story? Which one deserved God's favor? Which one earned God's favor? It is sometimes hard to tell the good guys from the bad guys. Two people came to Jesus one night. One kissed him and the other had a knife. The one who kissed him was a traitor and the one who used the knife was his best friend. Sometimes it is hard to tell who the good guys are. What this story is about is neither one of them were good guys. There is no good man in this story, there is no man, neither the Pharisee nor the tax collector, who earned and merited God's favor. Both men are dead. Dead in their sins as are you and I. We are dead in our sins. We are sinners. We have not earned one inch of God's favor or merit. We are just like they are. We are not looking for a heavenly bookkeeper, we are looking for a God who can raise the dead by His love and His grace. Both men needed mercy. Both men needed grace, as do we.

Someone has said there are only two kinds of people who pray. One person prays because it is the appropriate thing to do. The other person prays because lives depend upon it. You know it does. It does!

There is nothing wrong with being a drum major. I believe it was Frances Watson who has a statue or two in New York City and said at eighteen years of age I want to be somebody and I want to do something for somebody else. There is nothing wrong with leading a parade. There is nothing wrong with being successful, making our lives count, being meaningful to a world. There is nothing wrong with leading a parade if we are leading the right parade in the right direction.

One man did. His name is David Robinson. He played fourteen years in the NBA, two world championship rings, two Olympic gold medals, most valuable player, and all-star. David Robinson did everything in basketball that one could do and did so, as they said at his retirement party, "With class and dignity." He did not act fancy and silly and showboat after he made a good play. He did not leave the NBA littered with children that were his born out of wedlock. He was an example. The paper said that when he retired, "The good guys won." David Robinson won. Decency won! We all won. When he hoisted that trophy above his head he said, "Everybody in San Antonio knows what I am going to say." They did because they had heard him say it for fourteen years and this is what he said at the conclusion of his career, "God gets all the glory. For you see it is not about me. It is about God. It is all about God."

There are no good guys in this story. There are no good guys here. There is only one good guy and that is Jesus! It is Jesus! It is about God. It is about Jesus and what we can do to fit our lives into where Jesus is going today. That is what it is about. It is not about me. It is about Him and what I can do to be an instrument and a servant and to do what He wants me to do - to lead this church to do what God wants us to do. That is what it is about. That is what it is all about. Every time I think it is about me, I need to remember that in September 1954 when Ansel Baker issued the invitation to come and accept Christ they sang a hymn that day and the hymn said:

> Just as I am without one plea,
> But that thy blood was shed for me,
> And that thou bidds't me come to thee
> O, Lamb of God, I come. I come.

A Storyteller's Story
Philippians 4:13

A preacher needs to know his strengths and weaknesses. My weaknesses number more than a few. I've never been much of a pulpiteer, orator, or theologian. I guess if the good Lord gave me a strength. It might be that I'm a storyteller. I love stories. God has given me the gift to see stories in the everyday lives of people and the love of telling these stories that "my people" may see spiritual truth. Hopefully from my little stories they will be able to incorporate these spiritual truths into their own stories.

I'm a storyteller. I guess that's not too bad for fifty-nine years ago, someone told me a story. It was the greatest story ever told, and since I heard that story, I have never been the same. Now God has given me the glorious privilege of making it the business of my life to tell that wonderful story as I see it re-enacted in the lives of people just like you.

So if you haven't guessed it by now, I want to tell you a story. It's a true story about an old man I once knew. Oh what an old man he was! He taught me that God is our strength in hard going and that God uses our faithfulness for generations to come. Now that's quite a lot to learn from one old man, but listen to my story and see if you don't agree.

Times were bad and life was hard for a motherless young man growing up in rural America around the turn of the 20th century. Living with a hard and cruel father, he soon took on the character of his' home environment. He never went any- where without a gun and at least once, had used it in the direction of another human being. His father was prone to violence. Affidavits were later sworn to by family members that his father had beaten him severely on several occasions, once until "blood gushed in his boots." Bad turned to worse as he was forced at fifteen by his father to marry a woman several years his senior, whom he hardly knew. To put it discreetly, it soon became evident that the "marriage" was more for his father's access and convenience than it was for his.

After lying awake one night and overhearing his wife and his father plotting his murder, he left home. Let me quickly add that as cruel as his father had been to him, I personally never heard him say one unkind word toward his father. My information came from other sources. After leaving home, life was a series of misadventures and hard tasks. Then he met a young Christian woman in her mid-teens. She had to quit school after third grade to help raise her motherless brothers and sisters. So they shared a common predicament.

She had little. He had nothing. Soon after his divorce from his first wife, they were married. Being a godly woman, her influence was evident as he was soon saved and ordained a deacon in the Baptist church. Not long afterwards he acknowledged his calling to preach. Armed with little education but a great love for each other and the Lord, the young couple set out upon a road of hard going.

It was a struggle - hard going all the way. They parented six children. One died of diabetes and two more were claimed in a flu epidemic. All three would probably be saved today. To feed and clothe this large family he worked a wide variety of jobs. He worked as a miner, carpenter, and farmer, among others. There was never an abundance but always enough to share. More than one weary transient or hobo was told, "Go down to the preacher's house and knock on the back door. There will always be a meal for you there. More often than not the meal also included a night's lodging, free of course. No one was ever turned away. Their humble home was opened to all.

One particular occasion when the going was hard and at the height of the Depression, he was selling photographs in an effort to keep his family together. Upon calling on a young woman to deliver her pictures, he found that she had been recently widowed. Several small children cluttered the house. Nothing would do her but to spend the last dollars in the house to pay for the photographs of her deceased husband. He reluctantly accepted the money. Within hours he and his black-haired, freckle-faced son had taken the money, bought food, and delivered the groceries to the surprised widow. He didn't keep that job long for he kept giving away the profits.

They continued to struggle but hard going did not dull his keen wit and quick sense of humor. He loved people, especially children, and was particularly fond of practical jokes. He once placed a "For Sale" sign in his neighbor's yard while he was away for a while. The neighbor had inquiries for days afterwards. On another occasion after she had stayed in the house for weeks to conceal the fact, he placed an ad in the local newspaper congratulating his daughter-in-law on her first set of false teeth. His best one was when he hid in the woods at the end of his neighbor's cornfield. As his neighbor made the turn with his mule and headed away from the woods, he spoke slowly in a heavenly voice, "Go preach my Word!" His neighbor froze in fear. He actually thought it was the voice of God. He slowly turned around only to see nothing. He returned to his plowing slowly and cautiously. On the second turn, again the command came from the wood: "Go preach my Word." After initially freezing again, the neighbor headed expediently toward the barn. The neighbor was never told anything different. Amid the hard going, there was always laughter. Second only to his love for his Lord and his family was his love for preaching. He proclaimed the good news of his Savior for fifty-three years. He served as pastor of only four churches but helped to start several more. He never served a full time church that paid a "full time salary." If he was paid at all, it was usually a meal, a chicken, or some fresh vegetables. Most of his ministry was an itinerant one, preaching in over one hundred churches. Because he never drove an automobile he would walk miles and miles to a preaching appointment. During the Depression, he served a church that from his door was forty miles one way. Often he would pack a clean shirt, grab his Bible, and begin walking the night before in order to reach the church in time. He simply went where God led and was faithful to his task. I heard him preach only once. Ten people were present, most of them his own family. But he was faithful and delivered his message as if it were before thousands in a columned cathedral.

He had one very rare and special gift. Like Barnabas of old, he had the gift of encouragement and applied it liberally, especially to young men who were about to or had recently entered the ministry. He had the ability to see God working in others and to help them callout their gifts. As much joy as was his ministry to him, it, too, was not without hard going. Credit it to misguided zeal or well intentioned ignorance, but he was called down from the pulpit for "having two living wives." But he kept on, doing his best for his Lord.

The years passed. His simple life and singular calling never changed. When he wasn't preaching or farming, he would be found standing on the street corner telling stories and swapping knives. His life was simple and full. Everyone in the small town knew and loved the old preacher.

Sam Keen said of his father that he died only at the end of his life. It also was true of the old preacher. In his 74th year he took ill. Within a year and only at the end of his life, he went to be with his Lord. He died where he wished to die - at home. Complaints were not heard from his lips during his last days, only the comment that he "was not worthy" of all the fuss and concern made over him. He received several very small checks from the Baptist minister's retirement fund. He cried each time. It was as if all he ever expected was hard going. To it he returned hard work, faithfulness to task, love, and gratitude.

The old preacher's funeral was held near his home in the small brick church that he had built with his own two hands. It had been a labor of love as he and his "Mrs." brick by brick, created a lasting monument to their love for their Lord. They also gave the land and much of the materials for the small building.

The sanctuary was full and an equal number stood outside the church house for the old preacher's memorial service. It was said that there were eight preachers present, all of whom he had helped to start in the ministry - nine, if you included his own son. Six took part in the service itself. There were other preachers whose lives he had touched who could not come.

Also present at the funeral that day was an eighteen year old pallbearer. As he carried his beloved grandpa to this final earthly resting place, he carried in his pocket the last piece of mail he ever received from those dying hands. In shaky script the last line was clear. It read, "I have prayed if it is God's will to hear you preach God's word." I think he has for that eighteen year old grandson is now your author.

Quite a story? Quite an old man! I will never be what Grandpa was, but it is my prayer that I can be part of what he was -- to you! Remember Jesus is our strength in hard going and HE loves you!

(Preached in loving memory of Reverend John Edward Frank Carver)

About the Preacher

Gary L. Carver is the pastor of the First Cumberland Presbyterian Church in Chattanooga, Tennessee. He has also served as pastor of churches in Indiana and Alabama. Carver is a graduate of Samford University (B.A.) and the Southern Baptist Theological Seminary (M. Div. and D. Min.), and has done additional graduate study at the Candler School of Theology with Fred Craddock and Harvard Divinity School with Harvey Cox. Carver has had over 50 sermons and articles appear in a variety of church publications, including *The Review and Expositor*, *Preaching*, *Lectionary Homiletics*, and *The Abingdon Ministers Manual*. He is also the author of *Out From The Ordinary*, *Acting on the Absurd*, *Distinctively Different*, *Search for Serendipity* and *Living a Victorious Life* with Tom Garrison.

www.ingramcontent.com/pod-product-compliance
Lightning Source LLC
Chambersburg PA
CBHW072012110526
44592CB00012B/1274